THE AUSTRALIAN
Women's Weekly

If you only own one Chinese cookbook, then this is the one to have! We've gathered together and updated many of your old favourites, then added several popular newcomers to the mix. Plus, because it's no longer an effort to find all the right ingredients, making a family meal from this book is easy as can be. So season your wok, sharpen your cleaver and reach for Chinese Cooking Class.

Pamela Clark

Food Director

contents

woks and stir-frying

Once you've bought and seasoned your wok, you'll soon find that stir-frying the evening meal is not just quick but easy too.

Clockwise from above: prepare all ingredients prior to cooking; heating oil in wok before adding food; keeping the ingredients moving by shaking the wok.

which wok to buy?

Woks come in a variety of shapes, sizes and finishes, ranging from the traditional carbon-steel wok to cast-iron, stainless-steel, non-stick and electric. The traditional round-based woks are great for gas burners, while the flat-based woks are best used on electric stoves. Many woks are available from Asian food stores, while others can be found in department and kitchen specialty stores.

seasoning a wok

Stainless-steel and non-stick woks don't need seasoning. However, carbon-steel and cast-iron woks need to be seasoned before they're used for the first time.

First, wash the wok in hot soapy water to remove all traces of grease, then dry it thoroughly. Place the wok on the stove over high heat, add about 2 tablespoons of cooking oil, rub over entire inside surface of wok with absorbent paper. Continue heating the wok for about 10 to 15 minutes, wiping with more paper; cool. Repeat process twice. The wok is now ready to use.

After each use, wash the wok in hot soapy water; do not scrub with steel wool or harsh abrasives. Dry wok thoroughly by standing it over low heat for a few minutes, then rub or spray a thin layer of cooking oil over the entire surface of wok, before storing, to avoid rust.

With regular use, the inside surface will darken and become well seasoned. The older and more seasoned the wok becomes, the better it cooks.

wok burner Wok burners, portable gas burners and wok-holes for barbecues are all available.

Clockwise from top left: stainless-steel wok; anodised aluminium wok; carbon steel wok; enamel-coated cast-iron wok with a non-stick heavy-gauge carbon steel wok placed inside it.

wok chan A wok spatula or chan is a metal, shovel-like implement used for lifting, tossing and stirring food. Wooden spatulas are best used in non-stick woks as they don't scratch the surface.

stir-frying tips

- Prepare all ingredients before you start to cook.
- For best results, cut meat across the grain as thinly as possible. To do this, wrap meat tightly in plastic wrap, then partly freeze before cutting into wafer-thin slices.
- Heat the wok before adding the oil.
- Heat the oil before adding food.
- Stir-fry meat, poultry and seafood over high heat, in batches, so that the food will brown and seal quickly.
- It is important to keep lifting, stirring and moving ingredients in the wok while stir-frying – a wok chan or a wooden spatula is ideal.
- You should also shake the wok while stir-frying: to do this, hold the handle in one hand (wear an oven glove for protection against the heat) – you will soon coordinate the shaking and stir-frying actions.
- Stir-fry the food just before serving it.

marinades

- If marinating uncooked meat, poultry and seafood, always be sure that any reserved marinade used for a sauce or dressing is brought to the boil before serving.
- Always cover and refrigerate mixtures while they are marinating.

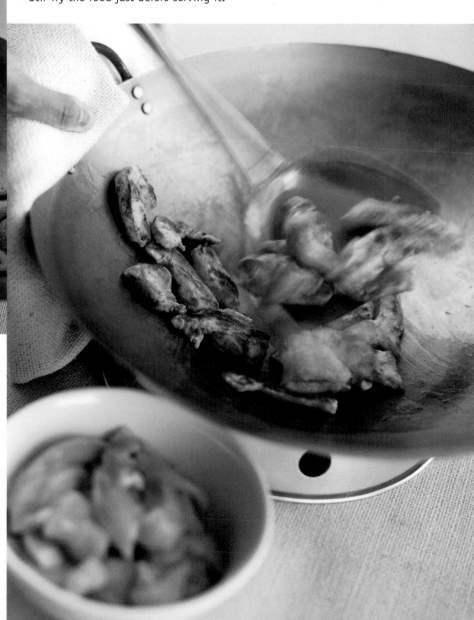

cooking and reheating rice

There are several methods of cooking rice – choose the one that suits your needs best.

absorption method

1 *Rinse uncooked rice until water runs clear.*

2 *Combine rice and water in saucepan, cover; bring to a boil.*

3 *Fluff cooked rice with a fork so that it doesn't "clump" while standing.*

BOILED METHOD

Bring water to a boil in a large saucepan, add rice, stir to separate grains; boil, uncovered, for recommended time or until rice is tender, then drain and fluff with a fork.

An electric rice cooker or a rice steamer will always give good, consistent results.

Do not rinse cooked rice unless specified in recipes.

ABSORPTION METHOD

Rinse uncooked rice until water runs clear. Combine water and rice in medium heavy-base saucepan. Cover tightly, bring to boil, reduce heat to as low as possible; cook for recommended time. Do not remove lid during cooking. Remove pan from heat; stand, covered, 10 minutes. Fluff rice with a fork.

MICROWAVE METHOD

Combine rice and boiling water in large microwave-safe bowl or jug. Cook, uncovered, on HIGH (100%) for recommended time or until rice is tender, stirring halfway through cooking. Remove from microwave oven, cover; stand 5 minutes. Fluff rice with a fork.

BAKED METHOD

Preheat oven to moderate. Combine rice and boiling water in ovenproof dish, stir well then cover tightly with foil or lid. Bake in moderate oven for recommended time or until rice is tender; fluff rice with a fork.

cooking times for rice

WHITE RICE *(long- and short-grain)*

method	quantity of rice	quantity of water	cooking time
absorption	1¹/₂ cups (300g)	3 cups (750ml)	10 minutes
microwave	1¹/₂ cups (300g)	3 cups (750ml)	10 minutes
baked	1¹/₂ cups (300g)	2¹/₂ cups (625ml)	25 minutes
boiled	1¹/₂ cups (300g)	8 cups (2 litres)	12 minutes

Note: we used an 830-watt microwave oven

white rice almost triples in bulk during cooking

rice advice

- 1 cup of uncooked white rice weighs 200g.
- White rice almost triples in bulk during cooking.
- Store uncooked rice, tightly covered, in a cool, dark place. Check the "use-by" date for a guide to suitable keeping times.
- Leftover cooked rice can be stored, covered, in the refrigerator for up to 2 days.
- Cooked rice freezes well. Place cooked rice in a freezer bag; press to remove air or use a freezer pump. Seal, date and label; freeze for up to 2 months.
- Quick-cook rice and ready-cooked frozen rice are convenient products when you are in a hurry; look for them in your supermarket.

reheating cooked rice

Reheating times will depend on the temperature and quantity of the rice.

- Place rice in metal colander. Place colander over saucepan of simmering water; cover, heat.
- Add just enough water to a frying pan to barely cover base. Bring to a boil, add rice, cover; heat until water is absorbed.
- Spread rice in a greased shallow ovenproof dish; sprinkle with a little water or milk, dot with butter. Cover, heat in moderate oven.
- Heat some butter or oil in a wok or frying pan, add rice, toss with a chan or a wooden spatula until hot.
- Place rice in a microwave-safe dish, cover; heat on HIGH (100%) in microwave oven.

soup and dim sum

Whether served as whole meals or appetisers, these subtly flavoured Chinese soups and more-ish dim sum "touch the heart" (as the words translate)... to say nothing of the tastebuds!

mongolian hot pot

PREPARATION TIME 30 MINUTES • COOKING TIME 20 MINUTES

The cooking vessel used for Mongolian hot pot can be purchased from Asian food stores. The pot is set in the centre of the table; guests add their own choice of food to the simmering stock. Small strainers, shown in picture, are for lifting the food from the stock into individual small bowls. When all the food has been eaten, the stock – which has now been transformed into a delicious soup – forms the last course.

250g beef fillet
250g pork fillet
350g chicken breast fillets
500g firm boneless white fish fillets
500g medium uncooked prawns
24 fresh oysters on the half shell (1.5kg)
230g can bamboo shoots, drained, sliced thinly
125g fresh baby corn
425g can straw mushrooms, drained, halved
1 medium carrot (120g), sliced thinly
300g Chinese cabbage, chopped coarsely
300g baby bok choy, chopped coarsely
1¹/₂ cups bean sprouts (120g)
125g snow peas
150g firm tofu, chopped
100g bean thread vermicelli
2.5 litres boiling chicken stock (10 cups)

1 Cut beef, pork, chicken and fish into very thin slices. Shell and devein prawns, leaving tails intact. Arrange beef, pork, chicken and seafood on serving plate.

2 Arrange remaining ingredients, except stock, on other serving plates.

3 Pour the boiling stock into the prepared hot pot. Serve with small bowls of light soy sauce, hoisin sauce and chilli sauce.

To prepare the hot pot Use heat beads sold for use in barbecues. The beads must be set alight, then burned until white hot; the best way to do this is in a barbecue or hibachi. While the heat beads are burning, stand the hot pot on a thick piece of wood to protect the surface on which the pot stands. Using tongs, quickly place the white-hot beads down the chimney of the hot pot.

SERVES 4 TO 6

tip An electric hot pot or a large electric frypan can be used instead of the traditional hot pot.

Cutting beef into thin slices

Chopping tofu

fried tofu soup
with shredded vegetables

PREPARATION TIME 15 MINUTES • COOKING TIME 10 MINUTES

1 medium carrot (120g)
100g snow peas
425g can baby corn, drained
1.5 litres vegetable or
  chicken stock (6 cups)
2 large red Thai chillies,
  chopped finely
2 green onions, sliced finely
1 tablespoon rice vinegar
2 tablespoons light soy sauce
150g baby bok choy, shredded
100g packaged fried tofu,
  sliced thinly

1 Cut carrot and snow peas into long thin shreds. Cut corn into quarters lengthways.

2 Bring stock to boil in large saucepan, add carrot, corn, chilli, onion, vinegar and sauce; simmer, uncovered, 2 minutes. Stir in snow peas, bok choy and tofu; cook, stirring, until bok choy is just wilted.

SERVES 4

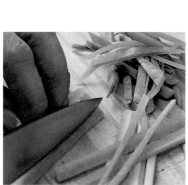

Shredding carrot and snow peas

Slicing tofu

Cutting pork into slices

Shredding Chinese cabbage

long soup

PREPARATION TIME 10 MINUTES • COOKING TIME 10 MINUTES

250g pork fillet
1.5 litres chicken stock (6 cups)
8 green onions, chopped finely
2 cups shredded Chinese
  cabbage (160g)
1 teaspoon grated fresh ginger
2 tablespoons light soy sauce
1 tablespoon dry sherry
125g thin fresh egg noodles
1/4 cup fresh coriander leaves
1/2 cup bean sprouts (40g)

1 Remove any fat and sinew from pork. Cut pork into thin slices, cut each slice into thin strips.

2 Bring stock to boil in large saucepan, add pork, onion, cabbage, ginger, sauce, sherry and noodles; simmer, uncovered, until noodles and pork are just tender. Ladle soup into serving bowls, top with coriander and sprouts.

SERVES 4

long and short soup

PREPARATION TIME 35 MINUTES • COOKING TIME 10 MINUTES

100g thin dried egg noodles
5 dried shiitake mushrooms
600g large uncooked prawns
2 litres chicken stock (8 cups)
1 cup finely shredded Chinese cabbage (80g)
2 tablespoons light soy sauce
1 tablespoon Chinese cooking wine
100g Chinese barbecued pork, sliced
4 green onions, sliced finely
1/2 cup bean sprouts (40g)
1 tablespoon finely chopped fresh coriander leaves

WONTONS

100g minced pork
1 clove garlic, crushed
1 teaspoon grated fresh ginger
1 tablespoon finely chopped fresh coriander leaves
2 teaspoons light soy sauce
12 wonton wrappers
1 egg, beaten lightly

Slicing shiitake mushroom caps thinly

Deveining prawns, leaving tails intact

Making wontons

1 Cook noodles in large saucepan of boiling water, uncovered, until just tender, rinse under cold water; drain. Place mushrooms in small heatproof bowl, cover with boiling water, stand 20 minutes; drain. Discard stems, slice caps thinly. Shell and devein prawns, leaving tails intact.

2 Bring stock to boil in large saucepan, add mushrooms, cabbage, sauce, wine and wontons; simmer, uncovered, 5 minutes. Add prawns; simmer, uncovered, until prawns just change colour. Stir in noodles, pork, onion, sprouts and coriander.

wontons Combine pork, garlic, ginger, coriander and sauce in medium bowl. Place rounded teaspoons of mixture in centre of wonton wrappers; brush edges lightly with egg. Bring opposite corners into centre of wonton wrapper, press along edges to seal.

SERVES 4 TO 6

Separating Hokkien noodles with a fork

Grinding lemon grass mixture

sichuan noodle soup

PREPARATION TIME 15 MINUTES • COOKING TIME 10 MINUTES

250g Hokkien noodles
1 teaspoon coarsely chopped fresh lemon grass
2 cloves garlic, quartered
1 teaspoon ground coriander
1¹/₂ teaspoons Sichuan peppercorns
1 teaspoon grated fresh ginger
1 tablespoon water
2 teaspoons peanut oil
1.25 litres beef stock (5 cups)
1 cup water (250ml), extra
200g beef rump steak, sliced thinly
170g chicken breast fillets, sliced thinly
2 teaspoons dark soy sauce
1 tablespoon coarsely chopped fresh coriander leaves
1 cup bean sprouts (80g)
¹/₂ cup fresh coriander leaves, extra

1. Rinse noodles under hot water; drain. Transfer to large bowl; separate noodles with fork.

2. Using a mortar and pestle (or a blender), crush lemon grass, garlic, ground coriander, peppercorns and ginger with the water and oil until mixture is well combined.

3. Cook lemon grass mixture in large saucepan, stirring, until fragrant. Add stock and the extra water, bring to boil; simmer, uncovered, 5 minutes. Add beef, chicken and sauce; simmer, uncovered, 5 minutes. Stir in noodles, chopped coriander and half of the sprouts. Ladle soup into serving bowls; top with remaining sprouts and coriander leaves.

SERVES 4 TO 6

chicken and corn soup

PREPARATION TIME 10 MINUTES • COOKING TIME 10 MINUTES

1.5 litres chicken stock (6 cups)
1 teaspoon grated fresh ginger
425g can creamed corn
1 teaspoon sesame oil
2 cups finely chopped cooked
**   chicken (340g)**
100g sliced ham, chopped finely
¼ cup cornflour (35g)
¼ cup water (60ml)
1 tablespoon light soy sauce
2 egg whites
2 tablespoons water, extra
3 green onions, sliced thinly

1 Bring stock to boil in large saucepan, add ginger, corn, oil, chicken and ham. Blend cornflour and water in small jug, stir in sauce; add to stock mixture, stir over heat until soup boils and thickens slightly.

2 Gradually add combined egg whites and extra water, in a thin stream, to simmering soup. Ladle soup into serving bowls; top with onion.

SERVES 4

Grating fresh ginger

Chopping cooked chicken finely

wonton soup with baby bok choy

PREPARATION TIME 20 MINUTES • COOKING TIME 10 MINUTES

1.5 litres chicken stock (6 cups)
1 tablespoon Chinese rice wine
1 tablespoon light soy sauce
1/2 teaspoon sesame oil
300g baby bok choy,
   shredded coarsely
2 green onions, chopped thinly
2 small red Thai chillies,
   cut into strips

WONTONS

150g minced chicken
2 green onions, chopped finely
2 teaspoons oyster sauce
18 wonton wrappers

1 Bring stock to boil in large saucepan, add wine, sauce, oil and wontons; simmer, uncovered, 5 minutes.

2 Add bok choy, onion and chilli; simmer, uncovered, until bok choy is just wilted.

wontons Combine chicken, onion and sauce in small bowl. Place rounded teaspoons of mixture in centre of wonton wrappers; brush edges lightly with a little water. Fold wrappers in half diagonally to form triangular wontons, pinch edges together to seal.

SERVES 4 TO 6

Making triangular wontons

Slicing shiitake mushroom caps thinly

Stirring egg white and water into soup

combination crab soup

PREPARATION TIME 20 MINUTES • COOKING TIME 15 MINUTES

5 dried shiitake mushrooms
1 teaspoon sesame oil
2 eggs, beaten lightly
1.5 litres chicken stock (6 cups)
8 green onions, chopped finely
1 teaspoon grated fresh ginger
1/4 cup canned bamboo shoots
   (50g), drained, sliced finely
200g cooked or canned crab meat
125g scallops
1/4 cup cornflour (35g)
1/4 cup water (60ml)
1 tablespoon light soy sauce
1 tablespoon Chinese
   cooking wine
2 egg whites, beaten lightly
2 tablespoons water, extra

1 Place mushrooms in small heatproof bowl, cover with boiling water, stand 20 minutes; drain. Discard stems, slice caps thinly.

2 Meanwhile, heat oil in wok or large frying pan, add eggs; swirl wok so eggs form a thin omelette over base, cook until set, remove, cool. Roll omelette, slice thinly.

3 Bring stock to boil in large saucepan. Add mushrooms, onion, ginger, bamboo shoots, shredded crab meat and scallops; simmer, uncovered, 2 minutes. Blend cornflour with the water in small bowl; stir in sauce and wine. Gradually add cornflour mixture to soup; stir gently over heat until soup boils and thickens slightly.

4 Just before serving, gradually add combined egg white and extra water in a thin stream to simmering soup; mix well. Stir in sliced omelette.

SERVES 4

deep-fried gow gees

PREPARATION TIME 40 MINUTES • COOKING TIME 10 MINUTES

Placing pork mixture onto wrapper

Folding and shaping gow gees

5 dried shiitake mushrooms
250g minced pork
4 green onions, chopped finely
1 tablespoon dry sherry
1 tablespoon hoisin sauce
1 clove garlic, crushed
1 teaspoon grated fresh ginger
150g baby bok choy, shredded, chopped finely
40 gow gee wrappers
1 egg, beaten lightly
vegetable oil, for deep-frying

CHILLI DIPPING SAUCE
2 tablespoons sweet chilli sauce
1 teaspoon light soy sauce
1 tablespoon Chinese rice wine
1 tablespoon water
1/2 teaspoon sugar

1 Place mushrooms in small heatproof bowl, cover with boiling water, stand 20 minutes; drain. Discard stems, chop caps finely. Combine mushrooms in medium bowl with pork, onion, sherry, sauce, garlic, ginger and bok choy.

2 Place rounded teaspoon of pork mixture in centre of each wrapper, brush edge lightly with egg. Fold in half; pinch to seal. Brush corners of gow gee with egg; press corners together. Repeat with remaining wrappers and pork mixture. Deep-fry gow gees, in batches, in hot oil until browned lightly and cooked through; drain on absorbent paper. Serve with chilli dipping sauce.

chilli dipping sauce Combine ingredients in small bowl.

MAKES 40

sang choy bow

PREPARATION TIME 20 MINUTES • COOKING TIME 15 MINUTES

The noodles used here are sold in supermarkets as "fried crispy egg noodles" in 100g cellophane bags.

4 dried shiitake mushrooms
1 tablespoon peanut oil
200g minced pork
200g minced chicken
6 green onions, chopped coarsely
1 clove garlic, crushed
1/4 cup canned drained bamboo
   shoots (50g), chopped finely
230g can water chestnuts,
   drained, chopped coarsely
2 teaspoons sesame oil
2 tablespoons light soy sauce
2 tablespoons oyster sauce
2 teaspoons cornflour
1 tablespoon dry sherry
100g fried noodles
1 cup bean sprouts (80g),
   chopped coarsely
2 green onions,
   sliced thinly, extra
8 large iceberg lettuce leaves

1 Place mushrooms in small heatproof bowl, cover with boiling water, stand 20 minutes; drain. Discard stems, chop caps coarsely.

2 Heat peanut oil in wok or large frying pan; stir-fry pork and chicken until cooked through. Add mushrooms, onion, garlic, shoots, chestnuts, sesame oil, sauces and blended cornflour and sherry; stir-fry 2 minutes. Just before serving, stir in noodles, sprouts and extra onion. Divide mixture among lettuce leaves, to serve.

SERVES 4

Chopping bamboo shoots finely

Removing leaves from iceberg lettuce

Folding gow gee wrappers in half

Deep-frying gow gees in batches

vegetarian gow gees

PREPARATION TIME 20 MINUTES • COOKING TIME 10 MINUTES

32 gow gee wrappers
1 egg, beaten lightly
vegetable oil, for deep-frying

FILLING
4 green onions, chopped finely
1 clove garlic, crushed
1 small carrot (70g), grated finely
1/2 cup finely shredded
** Chinese cabbage (40g)**
1 tablespoon hoisin sauce
1 tablespoon chopped fresh
** coriander leaves**
100g firm tofu, chopped finely

1 Place rounded teaspoon of filling in centre of each wrapper; brush edge lightly with egg. Fold in half; pinch to seal. Repeat with remaining filling and wrappers.

2 Deep-fry gow gees, in batches, in hot oil, until browned lightly and cooked through; drain on absorbent paper.

3 Serve gow gees with light soy sauce and fresh chopped chilli, if desired.

filling Combine ingredients in medium bowl; mix gently.

MAKES 32

stuffed chicken wings

PREPARATION TIME 40 MINUTES • COOKING TIME 50 MINUTES

12 large chicken wings (1.5kg)
3 dried shiitake mushrooms
500g minced chicken
1 tablespoon oyster sauce
1/4 teaspoon five-spice powder
4 green onions, chopped finely
2 cloves garlic, crushed
2 teaspoons grated fresh ginger
1 teaspoon sambal oelek
1 tablespoon cornflour

GLAZE
2 tablespoons oyster sauce
1 tablespoon honey
1 tablespoon dry sherry

Pushing meat down to middle joint of wing

Twisting and removing bones

Securing wing ends with toothpicks

1 Holding end of large third joint of wings, trim around bone with knife. Cut, scrape and push meat down to middle joint, without cutting skin. Twist bone and remove; discard bone. Using fingers, separate skin from bone of middle joint.

2 Place mushrooms in small heatproof bowl, cover with boiling water, stand 20 minutes; drain. Discard stems, chop caps finely.

3 Combine minced chicken with mushrooms and remaining ingredients in medium bowl; mix well. Using fingers, fill cavities of wings with mixture, secure ends with toothpicks.

4 Place wings, in single layer, in large oiled baking dish; cook, uncovered, in moderately hot oven about 50 minutes or until chicken is browned and cooked through, brushing with glaze occasionally during cooking.

glaze Combine ingredients in small bowl.

MAKES 12

Cutting lengthways along prawn backs

Gently flattening prawns on bread

prawns on toast

PREPARATION TIME 30 MINUTES • COOKING TIME 15 MINUTES

16 large uncooked prawns (800g)
2 eggs, beaten lightly
1/4 cup cornflour
8 slices thick white bread
1 green onion, chopped finely
vegetable oil, for deep-frying

SWEET CHILLI DIPPING SAUCE
1/4 cup sweet chilli sauce (60ml)
1/4 cup chicken stock (60ml)
2 teaspoons soy sauce

1 Shell and devein prawns, leaving tails intact. Cut along prawn backs, lengthways, without separating halves. Combine flattened prawns in medium bowl with egg and cornflour; mix well.

2 Remove and discard crusts from bread, cut each slice in half. Place one prawn, cut-side down, on each piece of bread, gently flatten prawn onto bread. Sprinkle prawns with onion, press on firmly.

3 Heat oil in wok or large frying pan; carefully lower prawn toasts, in batches, into hot oil. Deep-fry until browned lightly all over and cooked through; drain on absorbent paper. Serve with sweet chilli dipping sauce.

sweet chilli dipping sauce Combine ingredients in small bowl.

MAKES 16

marinated chicken sticks

PREPARATION TIME 40 MINUTES (plus marinating time) • COOKING TIME 25 MINUTES

12 large chicken wings (1.5kg)
1/4 cup light soy sauce (60ml)
2 cloves garlic, crushed
2 teaspoons grated fresh ginger
1 tablespoon brown sugar
2 tablespoons dry sherry
1 tablespoon peanut oil
2 tablespoons honey

1 Remove and discard tip from each wing; cut wings in half at joint. Holding small end of each piece, trim around bone to cut meat free; cut, scrape and push meat towards large end. One of the halves has an extra, thinner bone; remove and discard it.

2 Pull skin and meat down over end of bone; each wing piece will resemble a baby drumstick.

3 Mix chicken pieces with remaining ingredients in large bowl. Cover; refrigerate 3 hours or overnight.

4 Heat wok or large frying pan; cook undrained chicken, covered, 10 minutes or until chicken is almost cooked. Uncover, simmer, stirring occasionally, about 5 minutes or until chicken is browned and cooked through.

MAKES 24

Trimming around bone to cut meat free

Removing and discarding thinner bone

Pulling skin and meat over end of bone

spring rolls

PREPARATION TIME 30 MINUTES • COOKING TIME 10 MINUTES

18 spring roll wrappers
1 egg, beaten lightly
vegetable oil, for deep-frying

FILLING
2 dried shiitake mushrooms
250g uncooked prawns
2 teaspoons peanut oil
100g minced pork
1 clove garlic, crushed
1/2 cup finely shredded Chinese cabbage (40g)
1 small carrot (70g), grated finely
1 teaspoon grated fresh ginger
2 tablespoons oyster sauce

PLUM DIPPING SAUCE
2 tablespoons plum sauce
2 tablespoons water
1 tablespoon light soy sauce
1/2 teaspoon grated fresh ginger

Chopping mushroom caps finely

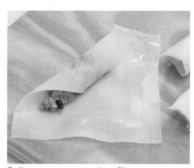

Rolling wrapper to enclose filling

1 Place level tablespoon of filling on a corner of each wrapper; brush edges lightly with egg, roll to enclose filling, folding in ends. Repeat with remaining filling and wrappers.

2 Deep-fry spring rolls, in batches, in hot oil, until browned lightly and cooked through; drain on absorbent paper.

filling Place mushrooms in small heatproof bowl, cover with boiling water, stand 20 minutes; drain. Discard stems, chop caps finely. Meanwhile, shell and devein prawns; chop prawns finely. Heat oil in wok or large frying pan, add pork and garlic; stir-fry until pork is browned lightly. Add mushrooms and prawns; stir-fry 1 minute. Add cabbage, carrot, ginger and sauce; mix well, cool.

plum dipping sauce Combine ingredients in small bowl.

MAKES 18

vegetarian rice paper parcels

PREPARATION TIME 30 MINUTES • COOKING TIME 5 MINUTES

2 dried shiitake mushrooms
150g firm tofu
8 round rice paper sheets
150g baby bok choy,
   shredded finely
1 green onion, chopped finely
1 tablespoon bottled fried onion

SOY DIPPING SAUCE

1 tablespoon light soy sauce
1 teaspoon Chinese rice wine
1/2 teaspoon sambal oelek
1/2 teaspoon sesame oil

1 Place mushrooms in small heatproof bowl, cover with boiling water, stand 20 minutes; drain. Discard stems, slice caps thinly. Slice tofu into 8 slices, combine in bowl with 2 teaspoons of the soy dipping sauce.

2 Place each rice paper sheet individually into a bowl of warm water for about 1 minute or until slightly softened; gently lift from water, place on board, pat dry with absorbent paper. Top each sheet with a slice of tofu, some bok choy, green onion and mushrooms. Fold rice paper over vegetables; fold in sides, fold over to make a parcel.

3 Place parcels, tofu-side up, in single layer, in baking-paper-lined bamboo steamer; cook, covered, over wok or large frying pan of simmering water about 5 minutes or until heated through. Serve accompanied by remaining dipping sauce and bottled fried onion.

soy dipping sauce Combine ingredients in small bowl.

MAKES 8

Softening rice paper sheet in water

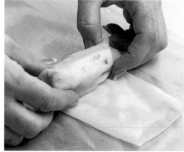

Folding rice paper over to make a parcel

Scoring squid hood

Stir-frying squid in batches

garlic and chilli squid

PREPARATION TIME 20 MINUTES (plus marinating time) • COOKING TIME 15 MINUTES

1kg squid hoods
2 teaspoons peanut oil
1/4 cup fresh coriander leaves
1 red Thai chilli, sliced

CHILLI PASTE

2 tablespoons peanut oil
4 cloves garlic, chopped
4 red Thai chillies, chopped
1 tablespoon grated fresh ginger
1 tablespoon white vinegar
1 tablespoon honey

1 Cut squid hoods in half; score shallow criss-cross pattern on inside surface, cut into 5cm pieces. Combine squid with the chilli paste in large bowl. Cover; refrigerate 3 hours or overnight.

2 Drain squid over medium bowl, reserve marinade. Heat oil in wok or large frying pan; stir-fry squid, in batches, until browned and tender. Add marinade to wok, bring to boil; simmer, uncovered, until mixture forms a thick glaze. Return squid to wok, stir through glaze. Serve on shredded Chinese cabbage, if desired; top with coriander and chilli.

chilli paste Blend or process ingredients until almost smooth.

SERVES 4

ham and chicken rolls

PREPARATION TIME 30 MINUTES • COOKING TIME 20 MINUTES

4 single chicken breast fillets (680g)
1/4 teaspoon five-spice powder
1 clove garlic, crushed
1 teaspoon sesame oil
2 green onions, chopped finely
4 slices ham
plain flour
1 egg, beaten lightly
1 tablespoon milk
4 large spring roll wrappers (21.5cm-square)
vegetable oil, for deep-frying

SWEET AND SOUR DIPPING SAUCE
1/3 cup sweetened pineapple juice (80ml)
1/4 cup water (60ml)
1/2 teaspoon brown sugar
1 tablespoon tomato sauce
1 tablespoon soy sauce
2 teaspoons white vinegar
1 teaspoon cornflour
1 green onion, chopped finely

Pounding chicken breasts

Rolling chicken to enclose ham

1 Using meat mallet, gently pound chicken breasts between sheets of plastic wrap until 5mm thick. Spread chicken with combined five-spice, garlic, sesame oil and onion. Roll 1 slice of the ham, place on a chicken breast; roll chicken breast, from long side, firmly around ham to enclose it, folding in ends as you roll. Repeat with remaining ham and chicken breasts.

2 Dip chicken rolls in flour, shake off excess; coat in combined egg and milk. Place one chicken roll diagonally across a spring roll wrapper, brush edges lightly with egg mixture. Fold in ends and roll to enclose chicken. Repeat with remaining chicken rolls and wrappers.

3 Deep-fry chicken rolls in hot oil about 10 minutes or until browned lightly and cooked through (do not have oil too hot or rolls will overbrown before cooking through). Drain on absorbent paper; cut diagonally into thick slices. Serve with sweet and sour dipping sauce.

sweet and sour dipping sauce Combine juice, water, sugar and sauces in small pan, add blended vinegar and cornflour; stir over heat until sauce boils and thickens slightly. Stir in onion.

SERVES 4 TO 6

Rolling chicken mixture into balls

Pleating wrapper firmly around chicken ball

steamed chicken gow gees

PREPARATION TIME 40 MINUTES (plus chilling time) • COOKING TIME 10 MINUTES

2 dried shiitake mushrooms
500g minced chicken
2 green onions, chopped finely
**1 tablespoon chopped fresh
   garlic chives**
2 cloves garlic, crushed
2 teaspoons grated fresh ginger
¹/₄ teaspoon five-spice powder
**³/₄ cup packaged
   breadcrumbs (75g)**
2 tablespoons hoisin sauce
1 teaspoon sesame oil
1 egg, beaten lightly
30 gow gee wrappers
**1 tablespoon Chinese
   barbecue sauce**
1 tablespoon light soy sauce
2 tablespoons water
2 teaspoons sweet chilli sauce

1 Place mushrooms in small heatproof bowl, cover with boiling water, stand 20 minutes; drain. Discard stems, chop caps finely.

2 Combine mushrooms, chicken, onion, chives, garlic, ginger, five-spice, breadcrumbs, hoisin sauce, oil and egg in large bowl. Roll level tablespoons of chicken mixture into balls (you will have 30 balls); place on trays. Cover; refrigerate 30 minutes.

3 Brush 1 wrapper with a little water, top with a chicken ball. Pleat wrapper firmly around ball. Repeat with remaining chicken balls and wrappers. Place gow gees, in single layer, about 2cm apart, in baking-paper-lined bamboo steamer. Cook, covered, over wok or large frying pan of simmering water about 8 minutes or until gow gees are cooked through.

4 Combine remaining ingredients in small bowl. Serve as a dipping sauce with gow gees.

MAKES 30

fish pouches with lemon sauce

PREPARATION TIME 20 MINUTES • COOKING TIME 10 MINUTES

**500g boneless firm white
 fish fillets, chopped
4 green onions, chopped finely
1 teaspoon grated fresh ginger
1 clove garlic, crushed
3 teaspoons Chinese
 barbecue sauce
24 spring roll wrappers
1 egg, beaten lightly
vegetable oil, for deep-frying**

LEMON DIPPING SAUCE

**2 teaspoons cornflour
2 tablespoons lemon juice
1 teaspoon light soy sauce
1/2 cup chicken stock (125ml)
1/2 teaspoon brown sugar**

1 Blend or process fish until it forms a paste. Combine fish paste in medium bowl with onion, ginger, garlic and sauce. Place 1 level tablespoon of fish mixture in centre of each spring roll wrapper, brush edges lightly with egg. Gather edges over filling into pouch shape; pinch to seal. Repeat with remaining fish mixture and wrappers.

2 Deep-fry pouches, in batches, in hot oil, until browned lightly and cooked through (do not have oil too hot or pouches will overbrown before cooking through); drain on absorbent paper. Serve with lemon dipping sauce.

lemon dipping sauce Blend cornflour with juice in small saucepan, stir in remaining ingredients; stir over heat until sauce boils and thickens slightly.

MAKES 24

Chopping fish fillets

Shaping filled wrappers into pouches

main meals

Given the innumerable variations on and nuances of Chinese main dishes, tossing up the possibilities for this chapter was a difficult (albeit delicious) task, but we're certain you'll go "yum" over our choices.

crab in black bean sauce

PREPARATION TIME 30 MINUTES • COOKING TIME 20 MINUTES

2 x 1.5kg uncooked mud crabs
1½ tablespoons packaged salted black beans
1 tablespoon peanut oil
1 clove garlic, crushed
1 teaspoon grated fresh ginger
½ teaspoon sambal oelek
1 tablespoon light soy sauce
1 teaspoon sugar
1 tablespoon Chinese rice wine
¾ cup chicken stock (180ml)
2 green onions, sliced diagonally

1 Place live crabs in freezer for at least 2 hours; this is the most humane way of killing a crab. Slide a sharp strong knife under top of shell at back of each crab, lever off shell and discard.

2 Remove and discard gills, wash crabs thoroughly. Chop body into quarters with cleaver. Remove claws and nippers, chop nippers into large pieces.

3 Rinse beans well under cold water, drain; lightly mash beans. Heat oil in wok or large frying pan; stir-fry garlic, ginger and sambal until fragrant. Add beans, sauce, sugar, wine and stock; bring to boil.

4 Add all of the crab; cook, covered, about 15 minutes or until crab has changed in colour. Place crab on serving plate; pour over sauce. Top with onion.

SERVES 4

Chopping crabs

Mashing beans with fork

prawns, choy sum and coriander

PREPARATION TIME 30 MINUTES • COOKING TIME 10 MINUTES

1.5kg large uncooked prawns
2 medium carrots (240g)
1 tablespoon peanut oil
1¹/₂ teaspoons chilli oil
1 tablespoon grated fresh ginger
¹/₄ cup honey (60ml)
¹/₄ cup rice vinegar (60ml)
4 green onions, sliced
300g baby choy sum, trimmed,
   shredded finely
2 tablespoons finely chopped
   fresh coriander leaves

1 Shell and devein prawns, leaving tails intact. Using a vegetable peeler, cut carrots into long thin strips.

2 Heat oils in wok or large frying pan; stir-fry prawns, in batches, until just changed in colour. Add ginger, honey and vinegar to same wok; bring to boil. Return prawns to wok with carrot, onion, choy sum and coriander; stir-fry until choy sum is just wilted.

SERVES 4

Shelling and deveining prawns

Cutting carrot into strips

Coating fish in flour mixture

Deep-frying fish

deep-fried fish with chilli vinegar sauce

PREPARATION TIME 15 MINUTES • COOKING TIME 20 MINUTES

**8 small firm white
    fish fillets (800g)**
1/3 cup light soy sauce (80ml)
3/4 cup cornflour (110g)
1/3 cup plain flour (50g)
11/2 tablespoons Sichuan seasoning
vegetable oil, for deep-frying
2 green onions, sliced thinly
**2 small red Thai chillies,
    sliced thinly**

CHILLI VINEGAR SAUCE

11/2 tablespoons hot chilli sauce
2 tablespoons tomato sauce
1 tablespoon light soy sauce
2 tablespoons water
3 teaspoons rice vinegar

1 Cut each fish fillet in half diagonally. Dip fish into soy sauce, drain off excess, then coat in combined flours and seasoning; shake off excess.

2 Heat oil in wok or large frying pan. Deep-fry fish, in batches, until browned all over and cooked through; drain on absorbent paper. Serve fish with chilli vinegar sauce, topped with onion and chilli.

chilli vinegar sauce Bring ingredients to boil in small saucepan.

SERVES 4

squid with chinese broccoli

PREPARATION TIME 15 MINUTES (plus marinating time)
COOKING TIME 15 MINUTES

1kg squid hoods
1/3 cup oyster sauce (80ml)
2 tablespoons Chinese rice wine
1 teaspoon sugar
1 teaspoon sesame oil
2 tablespoons peanut oil
2 cloves garlic, crushed
1 tablespoon grated fresh ginger
500g Chinese broccoli, chopped coarsely
6 green onions, sliced thinly
1 cup bean sprouts (80g)
1 tablespoon bottled fried garlic

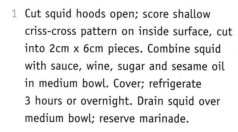

1 Cut squid hoods open; score shallow criss-cross pattern on inside surface, cut into 2cm x 6cm pieces. Combine squid with sauce, wine, sugar and sesame oil in medium bowl. Cover; refrigerate 3 hours or overnight. Drain squid over medium bowl; reserve marinade.

2 Heat half of the peanut oil in wok or large frying pan; stir-fry squid, in batches, until browned and tender. Heat remaining peanut oil in same wok; stir-fry garlic and ginger until fragrant. Add broccoli, onion and reserved marinade; stir-fry until broccoli is just tender. Return squid to wok; stir-fry until heated through. Toss in bean sprouts; serve topped with fried garlic.

SERVES 4

tip Fried garlic is available bottled from Asian food stores and some supermarkets – or you can make your own.

Scoring squid hood

Stir-frying squid

Soaking mushrooms

Adding scallops to stir-fry

scallop and vegetable combination

PREPARATION TIME 20 MINUTES • COOKING TIME 10 MINUTES

5 dried shiitake mushrooms
2 medium brown onions (300g)
1 tablespoon peanut oil
2 trimmed celery sticks (150g),
  sliced thinly
2 teaspoons grated fresh ginger
1 clove garlic, crushed
125g fresh baby corn
250g green beans, halved
1/2 cup chicken stock (125ml)
1 tablespoon dark soy sauce
2 teaspoons cornflour
1 tablespoon Chinese rice wine
500g scallops
300g bok choy, shredded

1 Place mushrooms in small heatproof bowl, cover with boiling water, stand 20 minutes; drain. Discard stems, slice caps thinly. Quarter onions; cut quarters into thin wedges. Heat oil in wok or large frying pan; stir-fry onion, celery, ginger, garlic and corn until onion is just tender.

2 Add mushrooms, beans, stock, sauce and blended cornflour and wine; stir-fry until sauce boils and thickens. Add scallops; stir-fry gently 2 minutes. Add bok choy; stir-fry gently until scallops are just opaque and bok choy is wilted.

SERVES 4

satay prawns

PREPARATION TIME 30 MINUTES (plus marinating time) • COOKING TIME 15 MINUTES

1.5kg large uncooked prawns
2 medium brown onions (300g)
2 teaspoons peanut oil
¼ cup chicken stock (60ml)
2 tablespoons finely chopped
** fresh coriander leaves**

MARINADE

¼ teaspoon five-spice powder
½ teaspoon sambal oelek
1 teaspoon mild curry powder
¼ cup satay sauce (60ml)
1 teaspoon light soy sauce
1 tablespoon dry sherry
1 teaspoon cornflour
1 teaspoon sugar

1 Shell and devein prawns, leaving tails intact. Cut lengthways along prawn backs, without separating halves. Combine prawns with marinade in large bowl. Cover; refrigerate 3 hours or overnight.

2 Quarter onions; cut quarters into thin wedges. Heat half of the oil in wok or large frying pan; stir-fry onion until just tender, remove from wok. Heat remaining oil in same wok; stir-fry undrained prawns, in batches, until browned lightly. Return onion and prawns to wok with stock; stir-fry until prawns are changed in colour and cooked through. Stir in coriander.

marinade Combine ingredients in small bowl.

SERVES 4

Shelling and deveining prawns

Cutting onion quarters into thin wedges

prawn omelette

PREPARATION TIME 20 MINUTES • COOKING TIME 30 MINUTES

2 dried shiitake mushrooms
500g medium cooked prawns
12 eggs
1/2 teaspoon five-spice powder
1 teaspoon sesame oil
1 cup bean sprouts (80g), chopped roughly
4 green onions, chopped finely
2 tablespoons peanut oil, approximately
1/4 cup fresh coriander leaves

SAUCE

1 teaspoon cornflour
1 tablespoon light soy sauce
2 tablespoons oyster sauce
1/2 cup water (125ml)

Soaking mushrooms

Cooking omelette

1 Place mushrooms in small heatproof bowl, cover
with boiling water, stand 20 minutes; drain.
Discard stems, chop caps finely. Shell and devein
prawns, halve lengthways. Whisk eggs, five-spice
and sesame oil in large bowl until combined. Stir
in mushrooms, prawns, sprouts and onion.

2 Brush 20cm non-stick frying pan with some of
the peanut oil, heat pan, pour about 1/2 cup
of the omelette mixture (125ml) into pan. Cook,
uncovered, until set underneath; turn, cook other
side. Remove omelette from pan, place on serving
plate; cover to keep warm. Repeat with remaining
oil and omelette mixture, layering and covering
cooked omelettes on serving plate. Pour sauce
over layered omelettes; top with coriander.

sauce Combine blended cornflour and sauces
with the water in small saucepan; stir over heat
until sauce boils and thickens.

SERVES 4 TO 6

honey prawns

PREPARATION TIME 30 MINUTES • COOKING TIME 15 MINUTES

1.5kg large uncooked prawns
1 cup self-raising flour (150g)
1¼ cups water (310ml)
1 egg, beaten lightly
cornflour
vegetable oil, for deep-frying
2 teaspoons peanut oil
¼ cup honey (60ml)
100g snow pea sprouts
2 tablespoons sesame
   seeds, toasted

1 Shell and devein prawns, leaving tails intact. Sift self-raising flour into medium bowl; gradually whisk in the water and egg until batter is smooth. Just before serving, coat prawns in cornflour, shake off excess; then dip into batter, one at a time, draining away excess.

2 Heat vegetable oil in wok or large frying pan. Deep-fry prawns, in batches, until browned lightly; drain on absorbent paper.

3 Heat peanut oil in same cleaned wok or large frying pan; heat honey, uncovered, until bubbling. Add prawns; coat with honey mixture. Serve prawns on snow pea sprouts, sprinkled with seeds.

SERVES 4

Coating prawns in cornflour then batter

Adding prawns to honey

steamed fish with chilli dressing

PREPARATION TIME 5 MINUTES • COOKING TIME 10 MINUTES

4 white fish cutlets (1kg)
2 tablespoons oyster sauce
1/4 cup peanut oil (60ml)
1 1/2 tablespoons rice vinegar
1 1/2 tablespoons sweet
  chilli sauce
1 teaspoon light soy sauce
1/4 teaspoon sugar
1/4 cup fresh coriander leaves

1 Place fish in bamboo steamer, drizzle with oyster sauce.

2 Cook, covered, over wok or large saucepan of simmering water about 10 minutes or until fish is just cooked. Whisk oil, vinegar, remaining sauces and sugar in small bowl. Serve fish drizzled with chilli dressing. Top with coriander leaves.

SERVES 4

tip Line steamer with baking paper to steam fish.

Steaming fish

Whisking dressing in bowl

baked fish
with ginger and soy

PREPARATION TIME 10 MINUTES • COOKING TIME 25 MINUTES

800g whole snapper
1 tablespoon grated fresh ginger
1 tablespoon peanut oil
1/4 cup Chinese rice wine (60ml)
1/4 cup light soy sauce (60ml)
1/2 teaspoon sugar
3 green onions, sliced thinly

1 Cut three deep slits in each side of fish, place fish in oiled baking dish.

2 Rub ginger into fish; drizzle with combined oil, wine, sauce and sugar. Bake, covered, in moderately hot oven about 25 minutes or until fish is cooked. Serve fish drizzled with some of the pan juices and topped with onion.

SERVES 2 TO 4

Cutting slits in fish

Drizzling fish with sauce mixture

braised prawns with vegetables

PREPARATION TIME 30 MINUTES • COOKING TIME 10 MINUTES

The noodles used here are called "fried crispy egg noodles" and are sold in 225g cellophane packets.

1kg large uncooked prawns
1 tablespoon peanut oil
1 teaspoon grated fresh ginger
250g broccoli, chopped
1 medium red capsicum (200g),
**   sliced thinly**
300g baby choy sum, trimmed,
**   chopped coarsely**
425g can straw mushrooms,
**   drained**
230g can sliced bamboo
**   shoots, drained**
2/3 cup chicken stock (160ml)
2 teaspoons cornflour
1 tablespoon Chinese
**   barbecue sauce**
1 tablespoon black bean sauce
225g packet fried noodles

1 Shell and devein prawns, leaving tails intact. Heat oil in wok or large frying pan; stir-fry prawns and ginger until prawns just change in colour.

2 Add vegetables, stock and blended cornflour and sauces; stir-fry until sauce boils and thickens slightly and prawns are cooked through. Serve prawn mixture over noodles.

SERVES 4 TO 6

Shelling and deveining prawns

Stirring in blended cornflour and sauces

spicy squid stir-fry

PREPARATION TIME 15 MINUTES • COOKING TIME 15 MINUTES

750g squid hoods
1 tablespoon Sichuan seasoning
1 medium brown onion (150g)
1¹/₂ tablespoons peanut oil
2 cloves garlic, crushed
2 tablespoons Chinese
    cooking wine
1 tablespoon Chinese
    barbecue sauce
100g snow pea sprouts
1 cup bean sprouts (80g)
¹/₄ cup fresh coriander leaves

1 Cut squid hoods open; score
   shallow criss-cross pattern on
   inside surface, cut into 2cm x
   6cm pieces. Combine squid with
   seasoning in medium bowl. Cut
   onion into thick wedges.

2 Heat 1 tablespoon of the oil in
   wok or large frying pan; stir-fry
   squid, in batches, until browned
   and tender. Add remaining oil
   to wok with onion and garlic;
   stir-fry until onion is just
   tender. Return squid to wok
   with wine and sauce; bring to
   boil. Just before serving, gently
   toss sprouts and coriander with
   squid mixture.

SERVES 4

Scoring squid hood

Stir-frying squid in batches

hokkien noodles with fried tofu and prawns

PREPARATION TIME 20 MINUTES • COOKING TIME 15 MINUTES

5 dried shiitake mushrooms
500g Hokkien noodles
300g packet firm tofu
vegetable oil, for deep-frying
1 tablespoon peanut oil
2 cloves garlic, crushed
2 teaspoons grated fresh ginger
500g large uncooked prawns, shelled
1/3 cup oyster sauce (80ml)
2 tablespoons light soy sauce
1 tablespoon hoisin sauce
1 tablespoon rice vinegar
300g baby choy sum, chopped
2 tablespoons sweet chilli sauce
2 tablespoons fresh coriander leaves

1 Place mushrooms in small heatproof bowl, cover with boiling water, stand 20 minutes; drain. Discard stems, slice caps thinly. Rinse noodles under hot water; drain. Transfer to large bowl; separate noodles with a fork.

2 Cut tofu into 2cm cubes. Heat vegetable oil in wok or large frying pan; deep-fry tofu, in batches, until browned all over, drain on absorbent paper. Heat peanut oil in same cleaned wok or large frying pan; stir-fry garlic, ginger and prawns until prawns just change in colour. Add noodles, mushrooms, sauces and vinegar; stir-fry until heated through. Add choy sum; stir-fry until just wilted. Serve noodles topped with tofu, chilli sauce and coriander leaves.

SERVES 4

Soaking mushrooms

Deep-frying tofu

lemon chicken tenderloins

PREPARATION TIME 15 MINUTES • COOKING TIME 15 MINUTES

¹/₂ cup cornflour (75g)
¹/₃ cup water (80ml)
4 egg yolks
700g chicken tenderloins
vegetable oil, for deep-frying
4 green onions, sliced thinly

LEMON SAUCE

1 tablespoon cornflour
1 tablespoon brown sugar
¹/₄ cup lemon juice (60ml)
¹/₂ teaspoon grated fresh ginger
1 teaspoon light soy sauce
¹/₂ cup chicken stock (125ml)

1 Place cornflour in medium bowl; gradually whisk in the water and egg yolks until smooth. Add chicken to cornflour mixture; mix well.

2 Just before serving, remove chicken pieces from batter, drain away excess. Heat oil in wok or large frying pan. Deep-fry chicken, in batches, until browned lightly and cooked through; drain on absorbent paper. Serve chicken drizzled with lemon sauce, topped with onion.

lemon sauce Blend cornflour and sugar with juice in small saucepan, add ginger, sauce and stock; stir over heat until sauce boils and thickens.

SERVES 4

Adding chicken to hot oil

Stirring sauce over heat

sesame chicken salad

PREPARATION TIME 15 MINUTES (plus cooling time) • COOKING TIME 15 MINUTES

4 single chicken breasts on
   bone (1kg), skin removed
1.5 litres chicken stock (6 cups)
2 star anise
1 tablespoon light soy sauce
1 teaspoon sesame oil
200g snow peas, halved
100g snow pea sprouts
2 cups bean sprouts (160g)
2 trimmed celery sticks (150g),
   sliced finely
4 green onions, sliced finely
1 tablespoon sesame
   seeds, toasted

DRESSING
2 tablespoons light soy sauce
1 tablespoon peanut oil
2 teaspoons sesame oil
1/2 teaspoon grated fresh ginger

1 Place chicken breasts in large saucepan, add stock, star anise, sauce and oil, bring to a boil; simmer, uncovered, 10 minutes. Cool chicken in stock, covered, drain over large bowl; reserve stock for another use. Remove chicken meat from bone; slice thickly.

2 Meanwhile, plunge peas into saucepan of boiling water, drain immediately; plunge into bowl of iced water for 2 minutes, drain.

3 Combine chicken with sprouts, peas, celery, onion and dressing in large bowl; top with seeds.

dressing Combine ingredients in screw-top jar; shake well.

SERVES 4

Slicing cooked chicken breast

Combining chicken and salad ingredients

honey chilli chicken

PREPARATION TIME 15 MINUTES • COOKING TIME 25 MINUTES

vegetable oil, for deep-frying
100g bean thread vermicelli
1 teaspoon chilli oil
3 teaspoons peanut oil
2 medium brown onions (300g), sliced thinly
4 cloves garlic, crushed
1 tablespoon grated fresh ginger
1kg chicken thigh fillets, halved
$^1/_2$ cup honey (125ml)
2 tablespoons sweet chilli sauce
500g Chinese broccoli, chopped roughly
$^1/_4$ cup roughly chopped fresh garlic chives

1 Heat vegetable oil in wok or large frying pan. Deep-fry noodles, in batches, until puffed and white; drain on absorbent paper.

2 Heat chilli oil and peanut oil in wok or large frying pan; stir-fry onion, garlic and ginger until fragrant. Add chicken, honey and sauce; stir-fry until chicken is browned and cooked through. Add broccoli and chives; stir-fry until broccoli is just tender. Serve over noodles.

SERVES 4

Deep-frying the noodles

Stir-frying only long enough to wilt broccoli

marinated chicken wing stir-fry

PREPARATION TIME 15 MINUTES (plus marinating time) • COOKING TIME 20 MINUTES

1kg chicken wings
3 cloves garlic, crushed
1 tablespoon grated fresh ginger
2 tablespoons hoisin sauce
2 tablespoons Chinese
  cooking wine
2 tablespoons honey
1 tablespoon peanut oil
230g can sliced bamboo
  shoots, drained
6 green onions, sliced thickly
300g baby bok choy,
  chopped coarsely

1 Remove and discard tip section from each wing; cut wings in half at joint. Combine wings in large bowl with garlic, ginger, sauce, wine and honey. Cover; refrigerate 3 hours or overnight.

2 Heat oil in wok or large frying pan; cook undrained chicken, covered, stirring occasionally, 10 minutes. Remove cover; stir-fry about 10 minutes or until chicken is browned and cooked through. Add shoots, onion and bok choy; stir-fry until bok choy is just wilted.

SERVES 4

Cutting wings in half at joint

Stir-frying chicken wings

spiced chicken

PREPARATION TIME 15 MINUTES (plus marinating and cooling time) • COOKING TIME 35 MINUTES

1.5kg chicken
2 litres chicken stock (8 cups),
   approximately
1/2 cup light soy sauce (125ml)
5cm piece fresh ginger, sliced
4 cloves garlic, sliced
1 tablespoon five-spice powder
1/2 cup Chinese barbecue
   sauce (125ml)
2 tablespoons dry sherry
2 teaspoons sesame oil
vegetable oil, for deep-frying

FRIED SPICE MIXTURE

1 tablespoon sea salt flakes
1 teaspoon cracked black pepper
1/4 teaspoon five-spice powder
1/4 teaspoon ground coriander

1 Place chicken in large saucepan, add enough of the stock to cover chicken; stir in soy sauce, ginger, garlic and five-spice. Bring to boil, reduce heat; simmer, uncovered, 10 minutes. Remove from heat, allow chicken to cool in stock, covered. Drain chicken on absorbent paper; discard stock. Using a large knife, poultry shears or cleaver, cut chicken in half through centre of breastbone, then cut on either side of backbone; discard backbone.

2 Coat chicken with combined barbecue sauce, sherry and sesame oil in large shallow dish. Cover; refrigerate 3 hours or overnight.

3 Heat vegetable oil in wok or large frying pan. Deep-fry undrained chicken, in batches, until browned all over and cooked through; drain on absorbent paper. Cut chicken into small serving pieces; serve with fried spice mixture.

fried spice mixture Cook salt and pepper in small saucepan, stirring, 2 minutes; add five-spice and coriander; cook, stirring, 1 minute.

SERVES 4

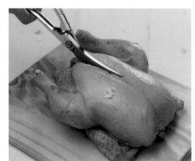

Cutting chicken in half

Cutting chicken into small serving pieces

ginger and green onion chicken

PREPARATION TIME 10 MINUTES (plus cooling and chilling time) • COOKING TIME 40 MINUTES

1.5kg chicken
2 litres chicken stock (8 cups), approximately
2 star anise
5cm piece fresh ginger, sliced thinly
1 clove garlic, sliced thinly
2 tablespoons light soy sauce
1 medium brown onion (150g), quartered
2 teaspoons Sichuan peppercorns

DRESSING

1/3 cup peanut oil (80ml)
1 tablespoon rice vinegar
1 teaspoon light soy sauce
1 tablespoon grated fresh ginger
2 green onions, chopped finely

Adding ingredients to chicken in pan

Cutting chicken into small serving pieces

1 Place chicken into large saucepan, add enough stock to cover chicken; stir in star anise, ginger, garlic, sauce, onion and peppercorns. Bring to a boil, reduce heat and simmer gently, uncovered, about 40 minutes or until chicken is very tender. Remove from heat; cool chicken in stock.

2 Drain chicken; reserve stock for another use. Cover chicken, refrigerate until firm and cold; cut into small serving pieces. Serve cold chicken drizzled with dressing. Top with fresh coriander leaves, if desired.

dressing Combine ingredients in screw-top jar; shake well.

SERVES 4

chicken and mango stir-fry

PREPARATION TIME 10 MINUTES • COOKING TIME 15 MINUTES

1 tablespoon peanut oil
600g chicken breast fillets,
   sliced thickly
1 tablespoon grated fresh ginger
1 clove garlic, crushed
1 tablespoon honey
1 teaspoon cornflour
1/2 cup chicken stock (125ml)
1 teaspoon sesame oil
2 medium mangoes (860g),
   sliced thickly
2 green onions, sliced thickly
100g snow pea sprouts
1 cup bean sprouts (80g)
1 tablespoon coarsely chopped
   fresh coriander leaves

1 Heat peanut oil in wok or large frying pan; stir-fry chicken, in batches, until browned lightly and just cooked through. Return chicken to pan with ginger and garlic; stir-fry until fragrant. Add blended honey, cornflour, stock and sesame oil; stir-fry until sauce boils and thickens.

2 Add mango and onion; stir-fry until heated through. Serve on combined sprouts; sprinkle with coriander.

SERVES 4

Cooking chicken in batches

Browning almonds in wok

Reheating chicken in wok

chicken and almonds

PREPARATION TIME 10 MINUTES • COOKING TIME 15 MINUTES

2 tablespoons peanut oil
1 cup blanched whole
   almonds (160g)
600g chicken tenderloins
1 teaspoon grated fresh ginger
2 tablespoons hoisin sauce
1 small leek (200g), sliced
200g green beans, halved
2 trimmed celery sticks
   (150g), sliced
2 green onions, chopped
1 tablespoon light soy sauce
1 tablespoon plum sauce
1 teaspoon sesame oil

1 Heat half of the peanut oil in wok or large frying pan; stir-fry almonds until browned, remove. Stir-fry chicken, in batches, in same wok until browned lightly and just cooked through.

2 Add remaining peanut oil and ginger to wok; stir-fry until fragrant. Add hoisin sauce, leek, beans and celery; stir-fry until beans are just tender. Return chicken to wok with onion, soy sauce, plum sauce and sesame oil; stir-fry until heated through. Toss through almonds.

SERVES 4

chicken chow mein

PREPARATION TIME 20 MINUTES • COOKING TIME 15 MINUTES

The noodles used here are sold in supermarkets as "fried crispy egg noodles" in 225g cellophane bags.

500g medium uncooked prawns
1 tablespoon peanut oil
500g chicken thigh fillets, sliced thinly
2 medium brown onions (300g), sliced thinly
2 cloves garlic, crushed
1 tablespoon grated fresh ginger
1 medium red capsicum (200g), sliced thinly
2 trimmed celery sticks (150g), sliced thinly
2 cups finely shredded Chinese cabbage (160g)
1/4 cup light soy sauce (60ml)
1 tablespoon oyster sauce
1 teaspoon sesame oil
2 teaspoons cornflour
1/2 cup chicken stock (125ml)
1 cup bean sprouts (80g)
6 green onions, sliced thickly
225g packet fried noodles

Shelling and deveining prawns

Combining capsicum, celery, onion and garlic

1 Shell and devein prawns, leaving tails intact. Heat half the peanut oil in wok or large frying pan; stir-fry chicken and prawns, separately, in batches, until chicken is browned and prawns just change in colour.

2 Heat remaining peanut oil in same wok; stir-fry brown onion, garlic and ginger until fragrant. Add capsicum and celery; stir-fry until vegetables are just tender. Return chicken and prawns to wok with cabbage, sauces, sesame oil and blended cornflour and stock; stir-fry until sauce boils and thickens. Add sprouts and green onion; stir-fry until heated through. Serve with fried noodles.

SERVES 4 TO 6

combination stir-fry

PREPARATION TIME 20 MINUTES • COOKING TIME 15 MINUTES

1 tablespoon peanut oil
500g chicken thigh fillets,
    chopped finely
250g minced pork
1 medium brown onion
    (150g), chopped
2 cloves garlic, crushed
2 teaspoons grated fresh ginger
1 large carrot (180g),
    chopped finely
500g medium uncooked prawns,
    shelled, deveined
300g Chinese cabbage, shredded
425g can baby corn, drained
230g can sliced bamboo shoots,
    drained, chopped finely
1 cup bean sprouts (80g),
    chopped coarsely
2 green onions, chopped coarsely
1 teaspoon cornflour
2 tablespoons light soy sauce
1 tablespoon black bean sauce

1   Heat half of the oil in wok or
    large frying pan; stir-fry chicken,
    in batches, until browned and
    cooked through. Heat remaining
    oil in same wok; stir-fry pork
    until browned. Add onion,
    garlic, ginger and carrot; stir-fry
    until onion is soft. Add prawns;
    stir-fry until prawns just change
    in colour.

2   Return chicken to wok with
    remaining vegetables and
    blended cornflour and sauces;
    stir-fry until cabbage is wilted.

SERVES 4

Chopping the bamboo shoots

Returning chicken to wok

billy kee chicken

PREPARATION TIME 10 MINUTES • COOKING TIME 20 MINUTES

1 teaspoon Sichuan seasoning
4 egg yolks
2 tablespoons cornflour
1kg chicken tenderloins
vegetable oil, for deep-frying
1/4 cup dry red wine (60ml)
1/4 cup tomato sauce (60ml)
1 tablespoon oyster sauce
1 tablespoon rice vinegar

1 Whisk seasoning, egg yolks and cornflour in medium bowl until combined; add chicken, mix well. Heat oil in wok or large frying pan. Deep-fry chicken, in batches, until browned and cooked through; drain on absorbent paper.

2 Bring wine, sauces and vinegar to a boil in wok or large frying pan; simmer, uncovered, 2 minutes. Add chicken; stir-fry until heated through.

SERVES 4

Deep-frying chicken

Tossing chicken with sauce

plum-glazed duck

PREPARATION TIME 10 MINUTES • COOKING TIME 1 HOUR 30 MINUTES

1.8kg duck
3 star anise
2 cloves garlic, peeled
5cm piece fresh ginger, sliced
2 cups water (500ml)

PLUM GLAZE
$^1/_3$ cup plum sauce (80ml)
2 tablespoons dark soy sauce
1 teaspoon sesame oil

1 Fill duck cavity with star anise, garlic and ginger; secure opening with toothpicks. Remove and discard the neck; tie legs loosely together with kitchen string. Place duck, breast-side up, on wire rack in large baking dish; pour the water into baking dish.

2 Roast duck, uncovered, in moderately hot oven 30 minutes. Baste duck all over with plum glaze; cover wing and leg tips with foil. Reduce heat to moderate; roast 30 minutes. Baste again with plum glaze, reduce heat to moderately slow; roast, covered loosely, about 30 minutes or until duck is tender and skin is crisp. Remove toothpicks and string.

3 Cut duck into small pieces to serve.

plum glaze Combine ingredients in small jug.

SERVES 4

Securing filled duck cavity with toothpicks

Covering wing and leg tips with foil

chicken hot pot

PREPARATION TIME 20 MINUTES • COOKING TIME 1 HOUR 45 MINUTES

Every time you want to cook in an Asian clay pot, submerge the pot in cold water for 24 hours.
When storing, always have a little water in the base to keep the pot moist.

5 dried shiitake mushrooms
1kg chicken thigh fillets, halved
2 cloves garlic, crushed
2 teaspoons grated fresh ginger
1 cup chicken stock (250ml)
1 tablespoon dark soy sauce
1 tablespoon oyster sauce
2 tablespoons Chinese
  cooking wine
1 tablespoon cornflour
2 tablespoons water
2 green onions, sliced thinly
1 tablespoon coarsely chopped
  fresh coriander leaves

1 Place mushrooms in small
   heatproof bowl, cover with
   boiling water, stand 20 minutes;
   drain. Discard stems, halve caps.
   Combine mushrooms with
   chicken, garlic, ginger, stock,
   sauces and wine in 1.25 litre
   (5-cup capacity) Asian clay pot
   or ovenproof dish.

2 Bake, covered, in moderate oven
   about 1½ hours or until chicken
   is very tender. Stir in blended
   cornflour and water; cook,
   uncovered, in moderate oven
   about 15 minutes or until sauce
   boils and thickens. Stir in onion
   and coriander.

SERVES 4

Soaking mushrooms

Adding coriander to pot

Slicing garlic and cutting onion

ginger garlic chicken with noodles

PREPARATION TIME 10 MINUTES • COOKING TIME 20 MINUTES

200g dried wheat noodles
1 teaspoon chilli oil
3 teaspoons peanut oil
500g chicken thigh fillets,
  sliced thickly
8 green onions, chopped coarsely
4 cloves garlic, crushed
2 tablespoons grated fresh ginger
600g baby choy sum, trimmed,
  chopped coarsely
2 tablespoons coarsely chopped
  fresh coriander leaves
2 tablespoons oyster sauce
2 tablespoons chicken stock

CRISP GARLIC AND GREEN ONION

4 cloves garlic, peeled
2 green onions
vegetable oil, for deep-frying

1 Cook noodles in large saucepan of boiling water, uncovered, until just tender, rinse under hot water; drain.

2 Heat oils in wok or large frying pan; stir-fry chicken, in batches, until browned all over and cooked through. Return chicken to wok with onion, garlic and ginger; stir-fry until fragrant. Add choy sum, coriander, sauce and stock; stir-fry until choy sum is wilted. Serve chicken mixture on noodles, topped with crisp garlic and green onion.

crisp garlic and green onion Cut garlic into thin slices, cut onion into 8cm long pieces. Heat oil in wok or large frying pan. Deep-fry garlic and onion, separately, in batches, until garlic is golden brown and onion is lightly browned and crisp; drain on absorbent paper.

SERVES 4

beggar's chicken

PREPARATION TIME 15 MINUTES • COOKING TIME 4 HOURS

The 1kg cooking salt in the dough recipe is correct. It does not affect the flavour of the chicken, but just ensures that the dough bakes rock-hard as protection for the chicken during the long cooking process.

1.5kg chicken
1 tablespoon dark soy sauce
2 tablespoons peanut oil
3 green onions, chopped finely
1 tablespoon grated fresh ginger
1 teaspoon sugar
1/4 cup light soy sauce (60ml)
2 tablespoons dry sherry
1/4 teaspoon five-spice powder

SALT DOUGH
4 cups plain flour (600g)
1kg coarse cooking salt
11/2 cups water (375ml), approximately

1 Place chicken on 2 large sheets of foil. Rub chicken all over with dark soy sauce, then brush with oil. Spoon combined onion, ginger, sugar, light soy, sherry and five-spice into chicken cavity; secure opening with toothpicks. Wrap chicken tightly in foil.

2 Roll salt dough on floured surface until large enough to completely enclose chicken. Place dough in oiled shallow baking dish. Place foil-wrapped chicken on dough; fold dough over and seal edges with a little water to completely enclose chicken. Bake, uncovered, in hot oven 1 hour; reduce heat to moderately slow, bake about 3 hours or until dough is brittle and crusty.

3 Remove chicken from oven; break salt crust with mallet and discard. Lift foil-wrapped chicken gently onto serving plate; carefully remove and discard the foil.

salt dough Place flour and salt in large bowl; stir in enough of the water to mix to a firm dough.

SERVES 4

Sealing chicken in salt dough

Breaking salt dough open

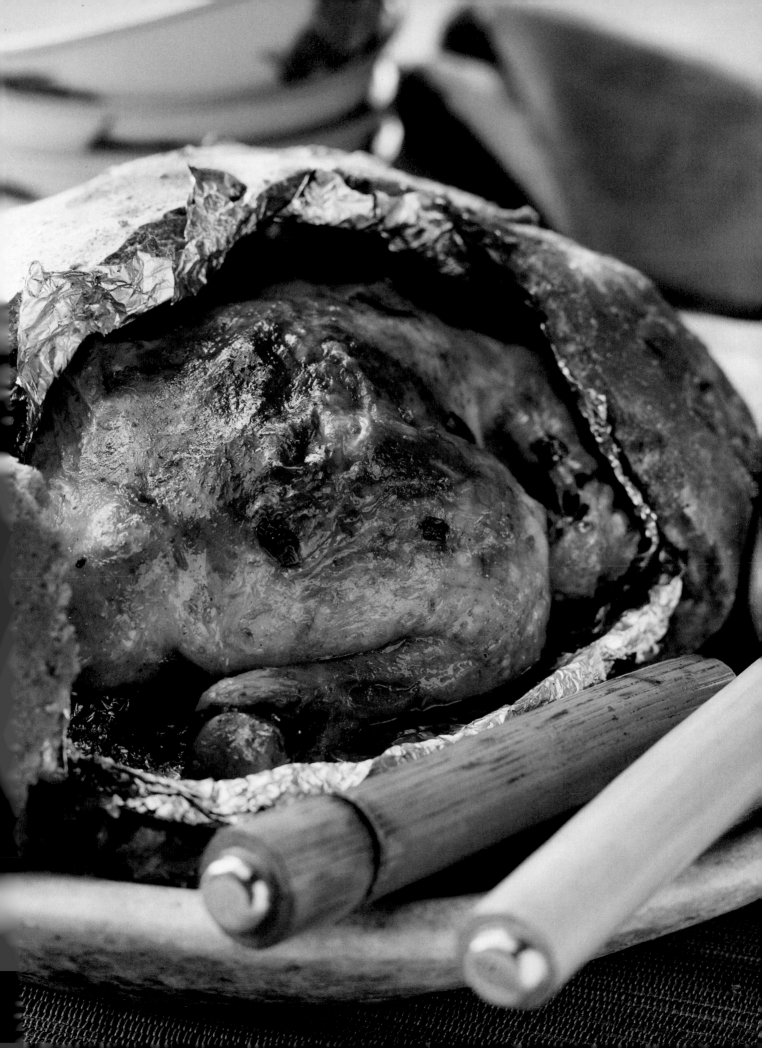

warm duck salad with noodles

PREPARATION TIME 15 MINUTES • COOKING TIME 10 MINUTES

1 Chinese barbecued duck
200g thin dried wheat noodles
2 green onions, sliced
100g snow pea sprouts
1 cup bean sprouts (80g)
1 bunch Chinese spinach
　　(450g), trimmed
230g can sliced water
　　chestnuts, drained
2 teaspoons dark soy sauce
1/2 cup flaked almonds
　　(40g), toasted

DRESSING
2 tablespoons hoisin sauce
1 tablespoon plum sauce
2 tablespoons rice vinegar
1/4 cup peanut oil (60ml)

1 Cut duck into small serving pieces. Cook noodles in large saucepan of boiling water, uncovered, until just tender; rinse under cold water, drain.

2 Combine noodles, onion, sprouts, spinach and chestnuts in large bowl with soy sauce and half the dressing. Serve duck pieces on noodle mixture; drizzle with remaining dressing, sprinkle with nuts.

dressing Combine ingredients in screw-top jar; shake well.

SERVES 4

tip English spinach can be substituted for the Chinese spinach.

Cutting duck into small pieces

Combining noodles with vegetables.

Cutting duck into small pieces

Grilling duck pieces, skin-side up

braised duck

PREPARATION TIME 20 MINUTES (plus standing time) • COOKING TIME 1 HOUR 50 MINUTES

5 dried shiitake mushrooms
1.8kg duck
4 star anise
1/2 teaspoon Sichuan peppercorns
2 cups chicken stock (500ml)
2 cloves garlic, sliced
1 teaspoon chopped fresh ginger
1 tablespoon Chinese barbecue sauce
2 tablespoons Chinese cooking wine
1 tablespoon cornflour
1 tablespoon water

1 Place mushrooms in small heatproof bowl, cover with boiling water, stand 20 minutes; drain. Discard stems, slice caps thinly. Meanwhile, cut duck into small serving pieces. Grill duck pieces, skin-side up, on wire rack placed over shallow oven tray, until skin is crisp and lightly browned and some fat has drained away; drain well on absorbent paper.

2 Tie the star anise and peppercorns in a small piece of muslin. Place duck and spices in 2-litre (8-cup) ovenproof dish; add mushrooms, stock, garlic, ginger, sauce and wine. Cook, covered, in moderate oven about 1 1/2 hours or until duck is very tender. Remove duck, cover to keep warm; remove and discard spices.

3 Skim off any fat from mixture in dish. Stir in blended cornflour and water; return to oven, cook, uncovered, about 15 minutes or until mixture boils and thickens slightly. Pour sauce over duck; serve topped with sliced green onion and coriander leaves, if desired.

SERVES 4

tip You can also use an Asian clay pot for this dish. Before using the pot, submerge it in cold water for 24 hours.

spicy chicken with cabbage and noodles

PREPARATION TIME 30 MINUTES (plus marinating time)
COOKING TIME 15 MINUTES

700g chicken breast fillets, sliced thickly
2 tablespoons rice vinegar
2 cloves garlic, crushed
1 teaspoon chilli oil
$1/2$ teaspoon five-spice powder
$1/4$ cup light soy sauce (60ml)
$1/4$ cup dried shrimp (30g)
500g Hokkien noodles
2 tablespoons peanut oil
300g Chinese cabbage, shredded finely
4 green onions, chopped finely
2 tablespoons finely chopped fresh garlic chives
2 tablespoons finely chopped fresh coriander leaves
50g snow pea sprouts

1 Combine chicken in medium bowl with vinegar, garlic, chilli oil, five-spice and 1 tablespoon of the soy sauce. Cover; refrigerate 3 hours or overnight.

2 Place shrimp in small heatproof bowl, cover with boiling water; stand 30 minutes, drain.

3 Rinse noodles in colander with hot water; drain. Transfer to large bowl; separate noodles with fork. Drain chicken over medium bowl; reserve marinade.

4 Heat peanut oil in wok or large frying pan; stir-fry chicken, in batches, until browned and cooked through. Return chicken to wok with reserved marinade; bring to a boil. Add noodles, remaining sauce, shrimp, cabbage, onion, chives and coriander; stir-fry until cabbage is just wilted. Toss in sprouts.

SERVES 4

Soaking shrimp in bowl

Rinsing Hokkien noodles

spicy beef fillet with bean sprouts

PREPARATION TIME 15 MINUTES (plus marinating time)
COOKING TIME 15 MINUTES

750g piece beef fillet
1 teaspoon light soy sauce
1 teaspoon sesame oil
1 teaspoon cornflour
1 tablespoon water
1¹/₂ tablespoons peanut oil
2 medium brown onions (300g), sliced thinly
1 clove garlic, crushed
1 teaspoon mild curry powder
1 tablespoon satay sauce
2 teaspoons light soy sauce, extra
1 teaspoon brown sugar
2 teaspoons dry sherry
2 tablespoons water, extra
1 cup bean sprouts (80g)

Flattening beef slices with mallet

1 Trim all fat and sinew from beef. Cut beef into 5mm-thick slices, flatten slightly with meat mallet. Combine beef in medium bowl with soy sauce, sesame oil, cornflour and the water. Cover; refrigerate 20 minutes. Heat 1 tablespoon of the peanut oil in wok or large frying pan; stir-fry beef, in batches, until browned both sides.

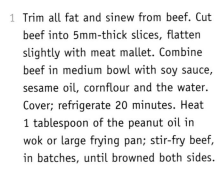

2 Heat remaining peanut oil in same wok; stir-fry onion, garlic and curry powder until fragrant. Add satay sauce, extra soy sauce, sugar, sherry and extra water; bring to boil. Return beef to wok; stir-fry until heated through. Toss in bean sprouts.

SERVES 4

Adding bean sprouts to wok

sichuan beef with choy sum

PREPARATION TIME 15 MINUTES (plus marinating time) • COOKING TIME 15 MINUTES

**500g piece beef fillet,
   sliced thinly**
2 tablespoons light soy sauce
**1 tablespoon Chinese
   barbecue sauce**
**2 tablespoons Chinese
   cooking wine**
1 clove garlic, crushed
2 teaspoons grated fresh ginger
1 teaspoon cornflour
1 tablespoon peanut oil
600g baby choy sum, trimmed
2 tablespoons oyster sauce
2 teaspoons peanut oil, extra
1 teaspoon sugar
**1 tablespoon Sichuan peppercorns,
   toasted, crushed**
4 green onions, sliced thinly
2 cups bean sprouts (160g)

1 Combine beef with soy and barbecue sauces, wine, garlic, ginger and cornflour in medium bowl. Cover; refrigerate 3 hours or overnight. Drain beef over small bowl; reserve marinade.

2 Heat peanut oil in wok or large frying pan; stir-fry beef, in batches, until browned.

3 Place choy sum in large heatproof bowl, cover with boiling water; stand 2 minutes. Drain choy sum, return to bowl with oyster sauce, extra peanut oil and sugar.

4 Return beef to wok with reserved marinade, peppercorns and onion; stir-fry until sauce boils. Add sprouts; stir-fry until just combined. Serve Sichuan beef on top of choy sum.

SERVES 4

Trimming ends from choy sum

Draining choy sum

cantonese-style fillet steak

PREPARATION TIME 15 MINUTES (plus marinating time) • COOKING TIME 15 MINUTES

750g piece beef fillet
2 teaspoons sugar
2 teaspoons cornflour
1 tablespoon light soy sauce
1 tablespoon oyster sauce
2 tablespoons dry sherry
2 medium brown onions (300g)
1¹/₂ tablespoons peanut oil
2 cups bean sprouts (160g)

1 Trim all fat and sinew from beef. Cut beef into 5mm-thick slices, flatten slightly with meat mallet. Combine beef in medium bowl with sugar, cornflour, sauces and half the sherry. Cover; refrigerate 3 hours or overnight.

2 Cut onions into thin wedges. Heat 2 teaspoons of the oil in wok or large frying pan; stir-fry onion until just tender, remove from wok. Heat half of the remaining oil in same wok; stir-fry beef, in batches, until browned both sides, adding remaining oil when needed. Return beef to wok with remaining sherry, onion and sprouts; stir-fry until combined.

SERVES 4

Flattening beef slices with mallet

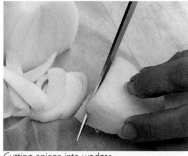

Cutting onions into wedges

beef and green beans

PREPARATION TIME 10 MINUTES • COOKING TIME 15 MINUTES

750g beef rump steak
1 clove garlic, crushed
1 tablespoon peanut oil
1 teaspoon chilli oil
2 tablespoons dark soy sauce
1 tablespoon black bean sauce
1 teaspoon brown sugar
2 teaspoons cornflour
1/2 cup chicken stock (125ml)
150g green beans, trimmed, halved
1 medium red capsicum (200g), sliced thinly
300g baby bok choy, chopped

1 Cut beef into thin slices. Combine beef with garlic and oils in
  medium bowl. Heat wok or large frying pan; stir-fry beef, in batches,
  until browned.

2 Add sauces, sugar and blended cornflour and stock to same wok;
  stir-fry until sauce boils and thickens. Add beans; stir-fry 2 minutes.
  Return beef to wok with capsicum and bok choy; stir-fry until bok choy
  is just wilted.

SERVES 4

Thinly slicing beef

Cutting beans in half

Cutting beef into slices, then strips

Browning beef in wok

sherried beef with choy sum

PREPARATION TIME 10 MINUTES (plus marinating time) • COOKING TIME 10 MINUTES

500g piece beef fillet
1 teaspoon sesame oil
1 teaspoon Sichuan seasoning
2 tablespoons dry sherry
1 tablespoon peanut oil
2 teaspoons grated fresh ginger
2 tablespoons light soy sauce
1 tablespoon black bean sauce
1 teaspoon cornflour
1/3 cup chicken stock (80ml)
500g choy sum, trimmed, chopped

1 Cut beef into thin slices; cut slices into strips. Combine beef with sesame oil, seasoning and sherry in medium bowl. Cover; refrigerate 3 hours or overnight.

2 Heat peanut oil in wok or large frying pan; stir-fry beef mixture, in batches, until browned all over. Return beef to wok with ginger; stir-fry until fragrant. Add sauces and blended cornflour and stock; stir-fry until sauce boils and thickens. Add choy sum; stir-fry until just wilted.

SERVES 4

curried beef

PREPARATION TIME 15 MINUTES • COOKING TIME 15 MINUTES

2 medium potatoes (400g)
2 medium brown onions (300g)
2 tablespoons peanut oil
750g piece beef fillet,
** sliced thinly**
1 clove garlic, crushed
1 tablespoon mild curry paste
1 tablespoon satay sauce
1 teaspoon hot chilli sauce
1 tablespoon dark soy sauce
2 teaspoons cornflour
1/2 cup chicken stock (125ml)
1 tablespoon chopped fresh
** garlic chives**

1 Cut potatoes into 2cm cubes. Cut onions into thin wedges. Heat half the oil in wok or large frying pan; stir-fry beef, in batches, until browned all over.

2 Heat remaining oil in same wok; stir-fry potato until browned and almost tender. Add onion and garlic; stir-fry until onion is just tender. Add paste; stir-fry until fragrant. Add sauces and blended cornflour and stock; stir-fry until sauce boils and thickens. Return beef to wok; stir-fry until combined. Top with chives.

SERVES 4

Cutting onions into wedges

Stir-frying potato

spicy pork spareribs

PREPARATION TIME 10 MINUTES • COOKING TIME 30 MINUTES

1.5kg pork spareribs, chopped
1 tablespoon peanut oil
$1/4$ cup Chinese barbecue sauce (60ml)
2 tablespoons dark soy sauce
2 tablespoons sweet chilli sauce
2 cloves garlic, crushed
2 teaspoons grated fresh ginger
$1/4$ cup honey (60ml)
$1/3$ cup firmly packed brown sugar (75g)
$1/4$ teaspoon five-spice powder
$1/4$ cup dry sherry (60ml)

1　Cook spareribs in large saucepan of boiling water, uncovered, about 10 minutes or until just cooked; drain spareribs on absorbent paper, discard cooking liquid.

2　Heat oil in wok or large frying pan; stir-fry spareribs, in batches, until browned all over and cooked through, drain on absorbent paper. Drain oil from wok. Add sauces, garlic, ginger, honey, sugar, five-spice and sherry to wok, bring to a boil, add spareribs; stir-fry about 10 minutes, tossing until pork is well coated in thickened sauce.

SERVES 4

Boiling spareribs

Adding cooked spareribs to sauce

Shallow-frying pork

Scooping seeds out of cucumbers

sweet and sour pork

PREPARATION TIME 20 MINUTES • COOKING TIME 30 MINUTES

750g pork fillets
2 tablespoons hoisin sauce
cornflour
vegetable oil, for shallow-frying
440g can pineapple pieces in
    natural juice
2 Lebanese cucumbers (260g)
2 teaspoons peanut oil
1 medium brown onion (150g),
    sliced thinly
1 medium green capsicum (200g),
    chopped coarsely
2 trimmed celery sticks (150g),
    sliced thickly
2 tablespoons tomato sauce
2 tablespoons light soy sauce
1/4 cup white vinegar (60ml)
1 tablespoon cornflour, extra
1/4 cup chicken stock (60ml)

1 Cut pork into 1cm-thick slices, combine in medium bowl with hoisin sauce. Coat pork slices in cornflour, shake off excess. Shallow-fry pork, in batches, in hot vegetable oil until browned all over and cooked through; drain on absorbent paper.

2 Drain pineapple over small bowl; reserve juice. Halve cucumbers lengthways, scoop out and discard seeds using a spoon; cut cucumber into thick slices. Heat peanut oil in wok or large frying pan; stir-fry onion until just tender. Add capsicum and celery; stir-fry until just tender. Stir in reserved pineapple juice, tomato sauce, soy sauce, vinegar and blended extra cornflour and stock; stir-fry until sauce boils and thickens. Stir in pork, pineapple pieces and cucumber; cook until heated through.

SERVES 4

roast pork neck

PREPARATION TIME 5 MINUTES (plus marinating time) • COOKING TIME 1 HOUR 30 MINUTES

2kg piece pork neck
1/4 cup light soy sauce (60ml)
2 tablespoons dry sherry
1 tablespoon brown sugar
1 tablespoon honey
1 teaspoon red food colouring
1 clove garlic, crushed
1/2 teaspoon five-spice powder

1 Halve pork neck lengthways. Combine pork in large bowl with remaining ingredients. Cover; refrigerate 3 hours or overnight. Drain pork over medium bowl; reserve marinade.

2 Place pork on wire rack over baking dish. Roast, uncovered, in hot oven 30 minutes. Reduce heat to moderate, roast, uncovered, about 1 hour or until pork is browned and cooked through, basting occasionally with the reserved marinade. Stand pork 10 minutes before slicing.

SERVES 6

Halving the pork neck

Basting partially cooked pork

sizzling mongolian combination

PREPARATION TIME 20 MINUTES (plus marinating time) • COOKING TIME 15 MINUTES

This recipe can be served on a pre-heated cast-iron steak plate, if desired. To give the "sizzle" effect, drizzle about 1 tablespoon of dry white wine or stock over the Mongolian combination on the heated dish just before serving.

200g beef fillet, sliced thinly
200g pork fillet, sliced thinly
200g chicken thigh fillets, sliced thinly
2 teaspoons five-spice powder
2 teaspoons sugar
1 tablespoon cornflour
$1/3$ cup light soy sauce (80ml)
1 tablespoon black bean sauce
3 cloves garlic, crushed
$1^1/2$ tablespoons rice vinegar
1 egg, beaten lightly
500g medium uncooked prawns
250g squid hoods
2 tablespoons peanut oil
2 medium brown onions (300g), sliced thickly
$1^1/2$ tablespoons chicken stock
$1/4$ teaspoon sesame oil

Scoring inside surface of squid

Cooking seafood in batches

1 Combine beef, pork and chicken with five-spice, sugar, cornflour, half of the combined sauces, garlic, vinegar and egg in medium bowl. Cover; refrigerate 3 hours or overnight.

2 Drain beef mixture over small bowl; reserve marinade. Shell and devein prawns, leaving tails intact. Cut squid hoods in half; score shallow criss-cross pattern on inside surface, cut into 5cm pieces.

3 Heat half of the peanut oil in wok or large frying pan; stir-fry seafood, in batches, until browned all over. Heat remaining oil in same wok; stir-fry beef mixture, in batches, until browned all over. Add onion to wok; stir-fry until onion is just soft, remove. Add reserved marinade, remaining combined sauces, stock and sesame oil to wok; stir until sauce boils and thickens. Return seafood, beef and onion to wok; stir-fry until heated through.

SERVES 4 TO 6

pork in black bean sauce

PREPARATION TIME 15 MINUTES • COOKING TIME 15 MINUTES

1½ **tablespoons packaged**
   salted black beans
1 **tablespoon peanut oil**
750g **pork fillets, sliced thickly**
1 **clove garlic, crushed**
1 **teaspoon grated fresh ginger**
1 **teaspoon hot chilli sauce**
1 **tablespoon dark soy sauce**
1 **tablespoon oyster sauce**
½ **teaspoon sesame oil**
1 **tablespoon dry sherry**
1 **teaspoon sugar**
2 **teaspoons cornflour**
⅔ **cup chicken stock (160ml)**
2 **green onions, sliced thinly**

STIR-FRIED ONION AND SPROUTS

2 **medium brown onions (300g)**
2 **teaspoons peanut oil**
3 **cups bean sprouts (240g)**

1 Rinse beans under cold water for 1 minute, drain; mash beans lightly with fork in small bowl. Heat peanut oil in wok or large frying pan; stir-fry pork, in batches, until browned all over.

2 Add beans to same wok with garlic and ginger; stir-fry until fragrant. Add sauces, sesame oil, sherry, sugar and blended cornflour and stock; stir-fry until sauce boils and thickens slightly. Add pork and onion; stir-fry until pork is cooked as desired. Serve over stir-fried onion and sprouts.

stir-fried onion and sprouts
Cut onions into wedges. Heat oil in wok or large pan; stir-fry onion until just tender. Toss in bean sprouts.

SERVES 4

Mashing beans with fork

Adding sauces to bean mixture in wok

Soaking fresh rice noodles

Cooking omelette in wok

rice noodles with prawns and barbecued pork

PREPARATION TIME 20 MINUTES • COOKING TIME 20 MINUTES

600g fresh rice noodles
500g medium uncooked prawns
2 cloud ear mushrooms
1 teaspoon chilli oil
2 eggs, beaten lightly
2 tablespoons peanut oil
3 cloves garlic, crushed
1 tablespoon grated fresh ginger
1 tablespoon mild curry paste
2 tablespoons oyster sauce
**1 tablespoon Chinese
   barbecue sauce**
2 tablespoons dry sherry
¼ cup chicken stock (60ml)
**230g can water chestnuts,
   drained, sliced thinly**
**250g Chinese barbecued pork,
   sliced thinly**
4 green onions, chopped

1 Place noodles in large heatproof bowl, cover with boiling water, stand until just tender; drain. Shell and devein prawns, leaving tails intact. Place mushrooms in small heatproof bowl, cover with boiling water, stand 20 minutes; drain. Discard stems, slice caps thinly.

2 Heat chilli oil in wok or large frying pan; add egg, swirl wok so egg forms a thin omelette over base. Cook until set, remove omelette from wok; cool. Roll omelette; slice thinly.

3 Heat peanut oil in same wok; stir-fry garlic, ginger and paste until fragrant. Add prawns; stir-fry until prawns just change colour. Add mushrooms, noodles, sauces, sherry and stock; stir-fry until combined. Add omelette, chestnuts, pork and onion; stir-fry until heated through.

SERVES 4

gingered pork with vegetables

PREPARATION TIME 10 MINUTES (plus marinating time) • COOKING TIME 15 MINUTES

700g pork fillets
2 tablespoons grated fresh ginger
1/4 cup chopped fresh coriander leaves
2 tablespoons rice vinegar
2 tablespoons peanut oil
125g fresh baby corn, halved lengthways
1 medium red capsicum (200g), sliced thinly
100g snow peas, halved
2 tablespoons light soy sauce
250g spinach, trimmed
3 cups bean sprouts (240g)
1/2 cup fresh coriander leaves, extra

Slicing pork fillets thinly

Stir-frying corn, capsicum and snow peas

1 Slice pork fillets thinly, combine in medium bowl with ginger, coriander and vinegar. Cover; refrigerate 3 hours or overnight.

2 Heat half of the oil in wok or large frying pan; stir-fry pork mixture, in batches, until pork is browned and cooked through.

3 Heat remaining oil in same wok; stir-fry corn, capsicum and peas until just tender, remove from wok. Return pork to wok with sauce; stir-fry until heated through. Just before serving, gently toss cooked vegetables with pork, spinach, sprouts and extra coriander until spinach just wilts.

SERVES 4

sichuan pepper pork

PREPARATION TIME 10 MINUTES (plus marinating time) • COOKING TIME 15 MINUTES

2 teaspoons Sichuan peppercorns
600g pork fillets
2 cloves garlic, crushed
1 teaspoon chilli oil
1¹/₂ tablespoons peanut oil
450g baby bok choy, halved
1¹/₂ cups bean sprouts (120g)
2 tablespoons sweet chilli sauce
1 tablespoon light soy sauce

1 Toast peppercorns in small frying pan until fragrant. Using a mortar and pestle, crush peppercorns until finely ground.

2 Slice pork fillets thinly; combine in medium bowl with pepper, garlic and chilli oil. Cover; refrigerate 3 hours or overnight.

3 Heat 1 tablespoon of the peanut oil in wok or large frying pan; stir-fry pork mixture, in batches, until browned and cooked through. Heat remaining oil in same wok, add bok choy; stir-fry until just wilted. Return pork to pan with sprouts and sauces; stir-fry until heated through.

SERVES 4

Crushing peppercorns with mortar and pestle

Slicing pork thinly

barbecued pork chow mein

PREPARATION TIME 15 MINUTES • COOKING TIME 15 MINUTES

vegetable oil, for deep-frying
250g thin fresh wheat noodles
1 medium brown onion (150g)
1 tablespoon peanut oil
2 cloves garlic, crushed
2 teaspoons grated fresh ginger
1/4 teaspoon five-spice powder
2 trimmed celery sticks (150g),
  sliced thickly
1 medium carrot (120g),
  sliced thinly
200g Chinese cabbage,
  shredded finely
1 tablespoon black bean sauce
1 tablespoon oyster sauce
1 tablespoon soy sauce
300g Chinese barbecued pork,
  sliced thinly
2 tablespoons chopped fresh
  garlic chives

1 Heat vegetable oil in wok or large frying pan. Deep-fry noodles, in batches, until browned lightly and crisp; drain on absorbent paper.

2 Cut onion into thin wedges. Heat peanut oil in same cleaned wok; stir-fry onion, garlic, ginger and five-spice until fragrant. Add celery and carrot; stir-fry 2 minutes. Add cabbage, sauces and pork; stir-fry until cabbage is just wilted. Serve over noodles; sprinkle with chives.

SERVES 4

Deep-frying noodles

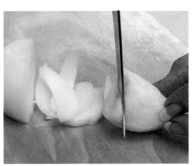

Cutting onion into wedges

spicy tofu with noodles

PREPARATION TIME 20 MINUTES • COOKING TIME 15 MINUTES

250g dried rice stick noodles
2 teaspoons chilli oil
6 green onions, sliced
2 cloves garlic, crushed
250g asparagus, chopped coarsely
1 small red capsicum (150g), sliced thinly
2 tablespoons sweet chilli sauce
2 tablespoons light soy sauce
1 tablespoon black bean sauce
1 tablespoon rice vinegar
1/4 cup vegetable stock (60ml)
190g packet fried tofu, chopped
500g spinach, chopped coarsely
1/3 cup unsalted roasted peanuts (50g)

Soaking dried rice stick noodles

Stir-frying vegetables

1 Place noodles in large heatproof bowl, cover with boiling water, stand until just tender; drain, rinse under cold water, drain.

2 Heat oil in wok or large frying pan; stir-fry onion, garlic, asparagus and capsicum until vegetables are just tender. Add noodles, sauces, vinegar and stock; stir-fry until sauce boils. Add tofu and spinach; stir-fry until spinach is just wilted. Serve topped with nuts.

SERVES 4

fried tofu and rice with spicy sauce

PREPARATION TIME 15 MINUTES (plus rice cooking time) • COOKING TIME 20 MINUTES

You will need to cook about 2 cups long-grain rice (400g) for this recipe.

300g firm tofu
vegetable oil, for deep-frying
2 tablespoons peanut oil
1 medium brown onion (150g),
  chopped finely
2 large red chillies, sliced thinly
2 cloves garlic, crushed
6 cups cooked white
  long-grain rice
300g baby bok choy,
  chopped coarsely
4 green onions, chopped
1/4 cup fresh coriander leaves
1/4 cup unsalted roasted
  peanuts (35g)

SPICY SAUCE

2 teaspoons Chinese barbecue sauce
1 tablespoon soy sauce
1 tablespoon sweet chilli sauce
2 tablespoons smooth
  peanut butter
1 tablespoon rice vinegar
1/3 cup vegetable stock (80ml)

1 Cut tofu into 2cm cubes. Deep-fry tofu, in batches, in hot vegetable oil, until browned all over; drain on absorbent paper.

2 Heat peanut oil in wok or large frying pan; stir-fry brown onion, chilli and garlic until onion is soft. Add rice, fried tofu, bok choy and green onion; stir-fry until bok choy is just wilted. Serve drizzled with spicy sauce, topped with coriander and nuts.

spicy sauce Combine ingredients in small saucepan, bring to a boil; simmer, uncovered, until sauce has thickened slightly.

SERVES 4

Deep-frying tofu

Chopping bok choy coarsely

vegetarian fried rice

PREPARATION TIME 20 MINUTES (plus rice cooking time) • COOKING TIME 20 MINUTES

You will need to cook about 2 cups long-grain rice (400g) for this recipe.

**6 cups cooked white
long-grain rice**
5 dried shiitake mushrooms
2 tablespoons peanut oil
**1 cup whole blanched almonds
(160g), chopped**
3 eggs, beaten lightly
1 teaspoon chilli oil
1 tablespoon grated fresh ginger
¼ teaspoon five-spice powder
**1 medium red capsicum (200g),
sliced thinly**
190g packet fried tofu, chopped
425g can baby corn, drained
**230g can water chestnuts,
drained, halved**
**300g baby choy sum,
shredded thinly**
1 teaspoon sesame oil
2 tablespoons black bean sauce
1 tablespoon light soy sauce

1 Spread rice over shallow tray, cover with cloth, refrigerate overnight.

2 Place mushrooms in small heatproof bowl, cover with boiling water, stand 20 minutes; drain. Discard stems, slice caps thinly.

3 Heat half of the peanut oil in wok or large frying pan; stir-fry nuts until browned lightly, remove. Reheat same wok; add egg, swirl wok so egg forms an omelette over base. Cook until omelette is set; remove, cool. Chop omelette into 2cm pieces.

4 Heat remaining peanut oil and chilli oil in same wok; stir-fry ginger and five-spice until fragrant. Add rice, mushroom, nuts, omelette, capsicum, tofu, corn, chestnuts, choy sum, sesame oil and sauces; stir-fry until choy sum is just wilted.

SERVES 4

Chopping fried tofu

Spreading cooked rice over shallow tray

accompaniments

So satisfying, imaginative and versatile is this selection of side-dish recipes that, if you choose to serve two or three of them together, they easily stand on their own merits to make a flavoursome light meal.

rice-stick noodles, asparagus and snake beans

PREPARATION TIME 15 MINUTES • COOKING TIME 5 MINUTES

200g dried rice stick noodles
150g snake beans
1 tablespoon peanut oil
4 green onions, chopped finely
2 teaspoons Sichuan seasoning
2 cloves garlic, crushed
2 teaspoons grated fresh ginger
2 tablespoons light soy sauce
2 tablespoons chicken stock
1 teaspoon sugar
1 tablespoon Chinese rice wine
250g asparagus, trimmed, halved
1 cup bean sprouts (80g)

Soaking noodles

Cutting snake beans

1 Place noodles in large heatproof bowl, cover with boiling water, stand until just tender. Rinse under cold water; drain.

2 Meanwhile, cut beans into 5cm lengths. Heat oil in wok or large frying pan; stir-fry onion, seasoning, garlic and ginger until fragrant. Add sauce, stock, sugar, wine, beans and asparagus; cook, covered, 2 minutes. Add noodles; stir-fry until heated through. Gently toss in bean sprouts.

SERVES 4

mixed green vegetables with cashews

PREPARATION TIME 10 MINUTES • COOKING TIME 5 MINUTES

150g snake beans
1 tablespoon peanut oil
1 medium brown onion (150g), sliced thinly
1 teaspoon grated fresh ginger
2 cloves garlic, crushed
250g broccoli, chopped coarsely
2 tablespoons chicken stock
500g choy sum, chopped coarsely
100g snow peas, halved
1 tablespoon black bean sauce
1 tablespoon light soy sauce
1/2 cup coarsely chopped cashews (75g), toasted

1 Cut beans into 5cm lengths. Heat oil in wok or large frying pan; stir-fry onion, ginger and garlic until fragrant. Add beans, broccoli and stock; cook, covered, 2 minutes.

2 Add choy sum, peas and sauces; stir-fry until choy sum is just wilted. Serve vegetables sprinkled with cashews.

SERVES 4

Cutting snake beans

Grating the fresh ginger

tossed green salad with peanuts

PREPARATION TIME 30 MINUTES

1/4 cup dried shrimp (30g)
500g Chinese water spinach,
   trimmed, chopped coarsely
2 cups coarsely shredded Chinese
   cabbage (160g)
2 cups bean sprouts (160g)
100g snow pea sprouts, halved
6 green onions, sliced thinly
200g snow peas, halved
230g can water chestnuts,
   drained, sliced thinly
1/2 cup unsalted roasted peanuts
   (75g), chopped coarsely

DRESSING
1 tablespoon peanut oil
1 tablespoon rice vinegar
1 tablespoon light soy sauce
1 teaspoon sugar

1 Place shrimp in small heatproof bowl, cover with boiling water, stand 30 minutes; drain.

2 Toss shrimp with spinach, cabbage, sprouts, onion, peas and chestnuts in large bowl. Drizzle salad with dressing; sprinkle with nuts.

dressing Combine ingredients in screw-top jar; shake well.

SERVES 4 TO 6

tip If Chinese water spinach is not available, substitute baby spinach leaves.

Soaking shrimp in water

Chopping Chinese cabbage coarsely

hot and sweet mixed vegetables

PREPARATION TIME 10 MINUTES • COOKING TIME 5 MINUTES

500g Chinese broccoli
1 tablespoon peanut oil
2 cloves garlic, crushed
1 tablespoon grated fresh ginger
300g tat soi, trimmed
300g baby bok choy, chopped coarsely
300g Chinese cabbage, chopped
2 tablespoons light soy sauce
1/4 cup Chinese barbecue sauce (60ml)
2 tablespoons sweet chilli sauce
1 1/2 cups bean sprouts (120g)

Trimming and chopping Chinese broccoli

Stir-frying all vegetables

1 Discard tough ends from broccoli; chop broccoli coarsely. Heat oil in wok or large frying pan; stir-fry garlic and ginger until fragrant.

2 Add broccoli, tat soi, bok choy, cabbage and combined sauces; stir-fry until vegetables are just tender. Toss in bean sprouts off the heat.

SERVES 4 TO 6

spinach with toasted almonds

PREPARATION TIME 10 MINUTES • COOKING TIME 5 MINUTES

1kg spinach
2 teaspoons peanut oil
2 tablespoons Chinese
** rice wine vinegar**
2 tablespoons light soy sauce
2 tablespoons honey
1 clove garlic, crushed
1 teaspoon grated fresh ginger
4 green onions, chopped thickly
1/2 cup flaked almonds
** (40g), toasted**

1 Trim spinach. Heat oil in wok or large frying pan, add vinegar, sauce, honey, garlic and ginger; bring to a boil.

2 Add spinach and onion; stir-fry until spinach is just wilted. Serve sprinkled with nuts.

SERVES 4

Trimming spinach

Boiling sauce ingredients in pan

rice noodles with baby bok choy

PREPARATION TIME 10 MINUTES • COOKING TIME 5 MINUTES

1kg fresh rice noodles
1 tablespoon peanut oil
1 teaspoon sesame oil
2 teaspoons grated fresh ginger
2 cloves garlic, crushed
700g baby bok choy,
   chopped coarsely
1/3 cup Chinese barbecue
   sauce (80ml)
1/3 cup chicken stock (80ml)
2 teaspoons sesame seeds, toasted

1 Place noodles in large heatproof bowl, cover with boiling water, stand until just tender; drain.

2 Heat oils in wok or large frying pan; stir-fry ginger and garlic until fragrant. Add bok choy, sauce and stock; stir-fry until bok choy is just wilted. Add noodles; stir-fry until noodles are heated through. Serve sprinkled with sesame seeds.

SERVES 6

Soaking fresh rice noodles

Chopping baby bok choy coarsely

noodles with asparagus and spinach

PREPARATION TIME 10 MINUTES • COOKING TIME 5 MINUTES

Rinsing Hokkien noodles

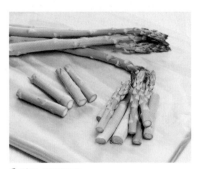

Cutting asparagus

500g Hokkien noodles
250g asparagus
1 tablespoon peanut oil
1 teaspoon grated fresh ginger
4 green onions, chopped finely
2 tablespoons dark soy sauce
1 tablespoon Chinese cooking wine
500g spinach, trimmed
1 tablespoon bottled fried garlic

1 Rinse noodles under hot water; drain. Transfer noodles to large bowl; separate noodles with fork.

2 Trim ends from asparagus; cut into 8cm lengths. Heat oil in wok or large frying pan; stir-fry asparagus, ginger and onion until fragrant. Add noodles, sauce, wine and spinach; stir-fry until noodles are heated through and spinach is just wilted. Serve topped with fried garlic.

SERVES 4 TO 6

mixed vegetable stir-fry

PREPARATION TIME 20 MINUTES (plus standing time) • COOKING TIME 5 MINUTES

3 dried cloud ear mushrooms
500g Chinese broccoli
1 tablespoon peanut oil
2 medium carrots (240g),
**   sliced thinly**
2 cloves garlic, crushed
230g can water chestnuts,
**   drained, halved**
230g can bamboo shoots, drained,
**   sliced thinly**
1 tablespoon oyster sauce
2 teaspoons satay sauce
1 teaspoon sesame oil
4 green onions, chopped finely
425g can baby corn, drained
2 cups bean sprouts (160g)
1 tablespoon finely chopped
**   fresh coriander leaves**

1 Place mushrooms in small heatproof bowl, cover with boiling water, stand 20 minutes; drain. Discard stems, slice caps thinly. Discard tough ends from broccoli; chop broccoli coarsely.

2 Heat peanut oil in wok or large frying pan; stir-fry carrot until almost tender. Add mushrooms, garlic, chestnuts, shoots, sauces, sesame oil, onion, corn and broccoli; stir-fry until broccoli is just tender. Add sprouts and coriander, off the heat; toss until combined.

SERVES 4

Soaking cloud ear mushrooms

Chopping Chinese broccoli

bok choy steamed with chilli oil

PREPARATION TIME 5 MINUTES • COOKING TIME 5 MINUTES

4 baby bok choy (600g)
1 tablespoon peanut oil
2 cloves garlic, crushed
2 tablespoons light soy sauce
1¹/₂ teaspoons hot chilli sauce
2 green onions, sliced
¹/₄ cup fresh coriander leaves
1 small red Thai chilli, seeded,
  sliced thinly

1 Halve bok choy lengthways; place, cut-side up, in bamboo steamer, drizzle with combined oil, garlic and sauces.

2 Steam bok choy, covered, over wok or large saucepan of simmering water about 5 minutes or until just tender. Serve bok choy sprinkled with onion, coriander and chilli.

SERVES 4

Halving bok choy lengthways

Steaming bok choy

combination fried rice

PREPARATION TIME 10 MINUTES • COOKING TIME 10 MINUTES

You will need to cook about 1¹/₃ cups long-grain rice (260g) for this recipe.

4 cups cooked white long-grain rice
2 teaspoons peanut oil
3 eggs, beaten lightly
1 tablespoon peanut oil, extra
2 cloves garlic, crushed
2 teaspoons grated fresh ginger
6 green onions, sliced thinly
200g cooked shelled small prawns
200g Chinese barbecued pork, sliced thinly
3 Chinese sausages (100g), sliced thinly
³/₄ cup frozen peas (90g), thawed
1 cup bean sprouts (80g)
2¹/₂ tablespoons light soy sauce

Spreading rice on tray

Cooking omelette

1 Spread rice over shallow tray, cover with cloth, refrigerate overnight.

2 Heat half of the oil in wok or large frying pan, add half the egg; swirl wok so egg forms an omelette over base. Cook omelette until set; remove, cool. Repeat with remaining oil and remaining egg. Roll omelettes, slice thinly.

3 Heat extra oil in same wok; stir-fry garlic, ginger and onion until fragrant. Add rice, omelette, prawns, pork, sausage, peas, sprouts and sauce; stir-fry until heated through.

SERVES 4

glossary

almonds
BLANCHED skins removed.
FLAKED paper-thin slices.
bamboo shoots the shoots of bamboo plants, available in cans.
beans
GREEN sometimes called French beans.
SNAKE long (about 40cm), thin, round green beans; Asian in origin.
bean sprouts also known as bean shoots; tender new growths of beans and seeds. The most readily available are mung bean, soy bean, alfalfa and snow pea sprouts.
beef
EYE-FILLET tenderloin.
RUMP STEAK boneless, tender, full-flavoured cut.
SCOTCH FILLET eye of the rib roast, rib-eye roll, cube roll.
bicarbonate of soda also known as baking soda.
black beans also called preserved black beans; salted, fermented soy beans. Sold in plastic packs or in cans with brine. Rinse in cold water and drain before using.
black bean sauce a Chinese sauce made from fermented soy beans, spices, water and wheat flour.
bok choy also called pak choi or Chinese white cabbage; has a mild mustard taste and is good braised or stir-fried. Baby bok choy is also available.
bread we used commercially sliced white bread.
breadcrumbs, packaged fine-textured, crunchy, purchased, white breadcrumbs.
broccoli should be cut in florets before cooking. Stems are just as tasty as florets but require longer cooking.

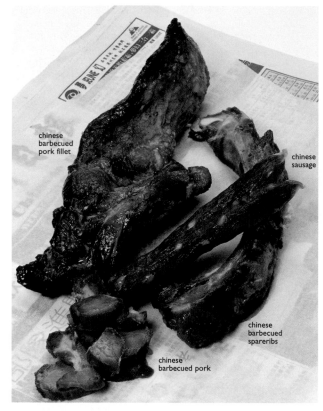

chinese barbecued pork fillet

chinese sausage

chinese barbecued spareribs

chinese barbecued pork

capsicum also known as bell pepper or, simply, pepper. Seeds and membranes should be discarded before use.
cashews we used unsalted roasted cashews.
chicken
BREAST whole, with skin and bone intact.
BREAST FILLET breast halved, skinned and boned.
MINCE minced breast and thigh meat.
TENDERLOIN thin strip of meat lying just under the breast.
THIGH FILLET thigh skinned and boned.
WING has skin and bones with a little meat.
chillies use rubber gloves when chopping fresh chillies as they can burn your skin. Removing seeds and membranes lessens the heat.

BIRDSEYE small red to orange fresh chillies; hot.
HOT CHILLI SAUCE we used a Chinese variety made from chillies, salt and vinegar.
POWDER the Asian variety is hottest; use as a substitute for fresh chillies in proportion of $1/2$ teaspoon ground chilli powder to 1 medium chopped fresh chilli.
SWEET CHILLI SAUCE mild, Thai-type sauce of red chillies, sugar, garlic and vinegar.
THAI small elongated fresh chillies, either red or green.
chinese barbecue sauce a thick, sweet and salty commercial sauce; made from fermented soy beans, vinegar, garlic, pepper and various spices. Available from Asian specialty stores.
chinese broccoli also known as gai larn.
chinese cabbage also known as Peking cabbage, Napa cabbage or wong bok.

chinese sausage highly spiced, bright-red, thin, dried pork sausage. The meat is preserved by the high spice content; can be kept at room temperature.
choy sum also known as flowering bok choy or flowering white cabbage.
coriander also known as cilantro or Chinese parsley; bright-green-leafed herb with a pungent flavour. Often stirred into a dish just before serving for maximum impact.
GROUND ground dried coriander seeds, sold in supermarkets.
corn
BABY tiny corn cobs; available canned in brine from Asian food stores or fresh from specialist greengrocers.
CREAMED available in various size cans from most supermarkets.
cornflour also known as cornstarch; used as a thickening agent in cooking.
crab
MEAT available canned, or from cooked fresh crabs. Also available, uncooked, frozen.
MUD we used uncooked mud crab, also called mangrove crab.
cucumber we used Lebanese (also known as European or burpless) cucumbers.
curry paste we used a mild, commercially prepared paste.
curry powder we used a mild-flavoured, commercially prepared powder.
duck
CHINESE BARBECUED sold whole or chopped, freshly cooked, in Asian food and barbecued meat shops.
WHOLE FRESH available from most specialty poultry shops.
five-spice powder fragrant mixture of ground cinnamon, cloves, star-anise, Sichuan pepper and fennel seeds.
flour
PLAIN an all-purpose flour, made from wheat.
SELF-RAISING plain flour sifted with baking powder in the proportion of 1 cup flour to 2 teaspoons baking powder.

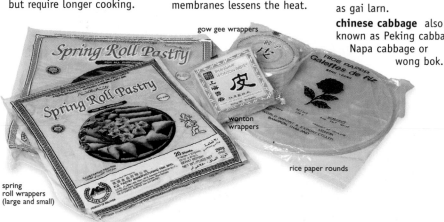

gow gee wrappers

wonton wrappers

rice paper rounds

spring roll wrappers (large and small)

canned straw mushrooms

dried cloud ear mushrooms

dried shiitake mushrooms

canned straw mushrooms

food colouring available in liquid, powder and paste forms; flavourless.

garlic chives also called Chinese chives, gau choy.

ginger, fresh also known as green or root ginger; the thick gnarled root of a tropical plant. Can be kept, peeled, covered with dry sherry in a jar and refrigerated, or frozen in an airtight container.

gow gee pastry we used 9cm rounds, available from Asian food stores; wonton or spring roll wrappers can be substituted.

hoisin sauce a thick, sweet and spicy Chinese paste made from salted fermented soy beans, onions and garlic; used as a marinade or baste, or to accent stir-fries and barbecued or roasted foods.

leek a member of the onion family, resembles the green onion but is much larger.

lemon grass tall, clumping, lemon-smelling and -tasting, sharp-edged grass; the white lower part stem is chopped and used in Asian cooking.

lettuce we used the heavy, round iceberg lettuce with its large, tightly packed leaves.

mangoes if fresh mangoes are unavailable, canned cheeks of mango in a light syrup could be used.

mushrooms

CLOUD EAR also known as wood ear or dried black fungus; sold dried, soak to rehydrate before use.

DRIED SHIITAKE have a meaty flavour; sold dried, soak to rehydrate before use.

STRAW cultivated Chinese mushroom with earthy flavour; sold canned in brine.

noodles

BEAN THREAD also known as cellophane or glass noodles; made from green mung bean flour. Thin and shiny, good softened in soups and salads or deep-fried with vegetables.

EGG made from wheat flour, water and egg; can be long thin strands or flat ribbons.

FRESH RICE wide, almost white in colour; made from rice and vegetable oil. Must be covered with boiling water to remove starch and excess oil before using in soups and stir-fries.

FRIED also known as crispy or crunchy fried noodles.

HOKKIEN also known as stir-fry noodles; fresh wheat noodles. Rinse under hot water, drain, separate with fork before use.

RICE also known as rice-flour or rice-stick noodles; made from ground rice. Sold dried; best deep-fried or soaked then stir-fried or used in soups.

oil

CHILLI made by steeping red chillies in vegetable oil, intensely hot in flavour; sold in Asian food stores.

PEANUT pressed from ground peanuts; most commonly used oil in Asian stir-fry cooking because of its high smoke point.

SESAME made from roasted, crushed, white sesame seeds; a flavouring rather than a cooking medium.

VEGETABLE any of a number of oils sourced from plants rather than animal fats.

onion

FLAKES packaged, chopped and dehydrated white onion pieces; must be reconstituted before use.

FRIED available bottled in Asian food stores; used mostly as a garnish.

GREEN also known as scallion or (incorrectly) shallot; an immature onion picked before the bulb has formed, having a long, bright-green edible stalk.

oyster sauce Asian in origin, this rich, brown sauce is made from oysters and their brine, cooked with salt and soy sauce, and thickened with starches.

peanut butter peanuts ground to a paste; available fresh or packaged.

peanuts we used unsalted, roasted peanuts.

plum sauce a thick, sweet and sour dipping sauce made from plums, vinegar, sugar, chillies and spices.

pork

CHINESE BARBECUED also known as char siew; roasted pork fillets with a sweet-sticky coating, available from Asian food and specialty stores.

FILLET skinless, boneless eye-fillet cut from the loin.

MINCED ground pork. Also known as pork scotch; boneless meat from a foreloin cut.

SPARERIBS cut from the pork belly then trimmed.

prawns crustaceans also known as shrimp.

rice

LONG-GRAIN elongated grain, remains separate when cooked.

RICE PAPER ROUNDS translucent sheets made from rice flour, water and salt; store at room temperature.

sambal oelek (also ulek or olek) Indonesian in origin; salty paste of ground chillies.

satay sauce we used a Chinese-style satay sauce.

scallops molluscs available with or without the coral (roe) attached.

sesame seeds seeds from the tropical plant *Sesamum indicum*. To toast, spread seeds evenly on oven tray, toast briefly in moderate oven.

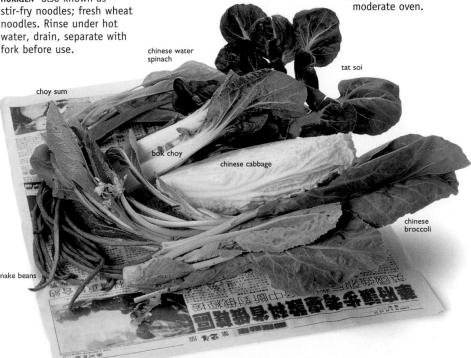

chinese water spinach

tat soi

choy sum

bok choy

chinese cabbage

chinese broccoli

snake beans

sherry fortified wine consumed as an aperitif or used in cooking; we used a dry sherry.

shrimp paste also known as trasi or blanchan; a pungent, almost solid, preserved paste made of salted dried shrimp.

sichuan pepper also known as Szechuan or Chinese pepper; red-brown aromatic seeds resembling black peppercorns, having peppery-lemon flavour.

sichuan seasoning powdered mix of garlic, salt, ginger, paprika, onion, pepper, chives, red pepper and spices.

snow peas also called mange tout ("eat all").

soy sauce made from fermented soy beans. Several variations are available in most supermarkets.

DARK used for colour as well as flavour.

LIGHT light in colour but generally quite salty.

spinach

CHINESE also known as yin choy, amaranth; sold with roots, which are pinkish red. Young shoots and leaves are the most tender.

ENGLISH correct name for spinach.

spring roll wrappers available in various sizes, fresh or frozen, from Asian food stores. Can be used for making gow gee and samosas as well as spring rolls.

squid hoods convenient cleaned squid (calamari).

star anise a dried star-shaped pod whose seeds have an astringent aniseed flavour.

stock 1 cup stock (250ml) is the equivalent of 1 cup water (250ml) plus 1 crumbled stock cube (or 1 teaspoon stock powder). If you prefer to make your own fresh stock, see recipes page 118.

sugar, brown extremely soft, fine granulated sugar retaining molasses for its characteristic colour and flavour.

tat soi also known as rosette bok choy, Chinese flat cabbage; variety of bok choy developed to grow close to the ground so it is easily protected from frost.

tofu soy milk "cheese". Several types are available in refrigerator cabinets of supermarkets and Asian food stores.

light soy sauce

chinese hot chilli sauce

oyster sauce

dark soy sauce

chinese rice vinegar

sweet chilli sauce

chinese cooking wine

plum sauce

hoisin sauce

chinese barbecue sauce

satay sauce

sambal oelek

FIRM made by compressing bean curd to remove most of the water.

FRIED packaged fried bean curd; bean curd cubes deep-fried until browned and crusty.

SOFT mainly used in soups.

vinegar

RICE also known as seasoned rice vinegar. Made from fermented rice; colourless, flavoured with sugar and salt.

WHITE made from spirit of cane sugar.

water chestnuts small, brown tubers with crisp, white, nutty-tasting flesh. Their crunchy texture is best experienced fresh, but canned water chestnuts are more easily obtained and can be kept about a month, once opened, under refrigeration.

wine Chinese cooking wine and Chinese rice wine are available from Asian food stores; substitute dry sherry if unavailable.

wonton wrappers gow gee, egg or spring roll pastry sheets can be substituted.

index

Making your own stock

These recipes can be made up to 4 days ahead and stored, covered, in the refrigerator. Be sure to remove any fat from the surface after the cooled stock has been refrigerated overnight. If the stock is to be kept longer, it is best to freeze it in smaller quantities.
All stock recipes make about 2.5 litres (10 cups).

BEEF STOCK

2kg meaty beef bones
2 medium onions (300g)
2 sticks celery, chopped
2 medium carrots (250g), chopped
3 bay leaves
2 teaspoons black peppercorns
5 litres water (20 cups)
3 litres water (12 cups), extra

Place bones and unpeeled chopped onions in baking dish. Bake in hot oven about 1 hour or until bones and onions are well browned. Transfer bones and onions to large saucepan, add celery, carrot, bay leaves, peppercorns and water; simmer, uncovered, 3 hours. Add extra water, simmer, uncovered, further 1 hour; strain.

CHICKEN STOCK

2kg chicken bones
2 medium onions (300g), chopped
2 sticks celery, chopped
2 medium carrots (250g), chopped
3 bay leaves
2 teaspoons black peppercorns
5 litres water (20 cups)

Combine ingredients in large saucepan, simmer, uncovered, 2 hours; strain.

FISH STOCK

1.5kg fishbones
3 litres water (12 cups)
1 medium onion (300g), chopped
2 sticks celery, chopped
2 medium carrots (250g), chopped
3 bay leaves
1 teaspoons black peppercorns

Combine ingredients in large saucepan, simmer, uncovered, 20 minutes; strain.

VEGETABLE STOCK

2 large carrots (360g), chopped
2 large parsnips (360g), chopped
4 medium onions (600g), chopped
12 sticks celery, chopped
4 bay leaves
2 teaspoons black peppercorns
6 litres water (24 cups)

Combine ingredients in large saucepan, simmer, uncovered, 1¹/₂ hours; strain.

Stock is also available in cans or tetra packs. Stock cubes or powder can be used. As a guide, 1 teaspoon of stock powder or 1 small crumbled stock cube mixed with 1 cup water (250ml) will give a fairly strong stock. Be aware of the salt and fat content of stock cubes and powders and prepared stocks.

facts and figures

Wherever you live, you'll be able to use our recipes with the help of these easy-to-follow conversions. While these conversions are approximate only, the difference between an exact and the approximate conversion of various liquid and dry measures is but minimal, and will not affect your cooking results.

dry measures

metric	imperial
15g	½oz
30g	1oz
60g	2oz
90g	3oz
125g	4oz (¼lb)
155g	5oz
185g	6oz
220g	7oz
250g	8oz (½lb)
280g	9oz
315g	10oz
345g	11oz
375g	12oz (¾lb)
410g	13oz
440g	14oz
470g	15oz
500g	16oz (1lb)
750g	24oz (1½lb)
1kg	32oz (2lb)

liquid measures

metric	imperial
30ml	1 fluid oz
60ml	2 fluid oz
100ml	3 fluid oz
125ml	4 fluid oz
150ml	5 fluid oz (¼ pint/1 gill)
190ml	6 fluid oz
250ml	8 fluid oz
300ml	10 fluid oz (½ pint)
500ml	16 fluid oz
600ml	20 fluid oz (1 pint)
1000ml (1 litre)	1¾ pints

helpful measures

metric	imperial
3mm	⅛in
6mm	¼in
1cm	½in
2cm	¾in
2.5cm	1in
5cm	2in
6cm	2½in
8cm	3in
10cm	4in
13cm	5in
15cm	6in
18cm	7in
20cm	8in
23cm	9in
25cm	10in
28cm	11in
30cm	12in (1ft)

measuring equipment

The difference between one country's measuring cups and another's is, at most, within a 2 or 3 teaspoon variance. (For the record, one Australian metric measuring cup holds approximately 250ml.) The most accurate way of measuring dry ingredients is to weigh them. When measuring liquids, use a clear glass or plastic jug with metric markings. (For the record, one Australian metric tablespoon holds 20ml; one Australian metric teaspoon holds 5ml.)

Note: NZ, Canada, US and UK use 15ml tablespoons. All cup and spoon measurements are level.

We use large eggs with an average weight of 60g.

how to measure

When using graduated metric measuring cups, shake dry ingredients loosely into the appropriate cup. Do not tap the cup on a bench or tightly pack the ingredients unless directed to do so. Level top of measuring cups and measuring spoons with a knife. When measuring liquids, place a clear glass or plastic jug with metric markings on a flat surface to check accuracy at eye level.

oven temperatures

These oven temperatures are only a guide. Always check the manufacturer's manual.

	°C (Celsius)	°F (Fahrenheit)	Gas Mark
Very slow	120	250	½
Slow	140 – 150	275 – 300	1 – 2
Moderately slow	170	325	3
Moderate	180 – 190	350 – 375	4 – 5
Moderately hot	200	400	6
Hot	220 – 230	425 – 450	7 – 8
Very hot	240	475	9

Are you missing some of the
world's favourite cookbooks?

The Australian Women's Weekly cookbooks are available from bookshops, cookshops, supermarkets and other stores all over the world. You can also buy direct from the publisher, using the order form below.

Title	RRP	Qty	Title	RRP	Qty
Almost Vegetarian	£5.99		French Food, New	£5.99	
Asian, Meals in Minutes	£5.99		Get Real, Make a Meal	£5.99	
Babies & Toddlers Good Food	£5.99		Good Food Fast	£5.99	
Barbecue Meals in Minutes	£5.99		Great Beef Cookbook	£5.99	
Basic Cooking Class	£5.99		Great Chicken Cookbook	£5.99	
Beginners Cooking Class	£5.99		Great Lamb Cookbook	£5.99	
Beginners Simple Meals	£5.99		Greek Cooking Class	£5.99	
Beginners Thai	£5.99		Healthy Heart Cookbook	£5.99	
Best Ever Slimmers' Recipes	£5.99		Indian Cooking Class	£5.99	
Best Food	£5.99		Italian Cooking Class	£5.99	
Best Food Desserts	£5.99		Japanese Cooking Class	£5.99	
Best Food Mains	£5.99		Kids' Birthday Cakes	£5.99	
Big Book of Beautiful Biscuits	£5.99		Kids Cooking	£5.99	
Biscuits & Slices	£5.99		Lean Food	£5.99	
Cakes & Slices Cookbook	£5.99		Low-fat Feasts	£5.99	
Cakes Cooking Class	£5.99		Low-fat Food For Life	£5.99	
Caribbean Cooking	£5.99		Low-fat Meals in Minutes	£5.99	
Casseroles	£5.99		Main Course Salads	£5.99	
Celebration Cakes	£5.99		Meals in Minutes	£5.99	
Chicken Meals in Minutes	£5.99		Mediterranean Cookbook	£5.99	
Chinese Cooking Class	£5.99		Middle Eastern Cooking Class	£5.99	
Christmas Book	£5.99		Midweek Meals in Minutes	£5.99	
Christmas Cooking (Oct 04)	£5.99		Muffins, Scones & Bread	£5.99	
Cocktails	£5.99		New Finger Food	£5.99	
Cooking for Crowds	£5.99		Pasta Cookbook	£5.99	
Cooking for Friends	£5.99		Pasta Meals in Minutes	£5.99	
Cooking for Two	£5.99		Potatoes	£5.99	
Creative Cooking on a Budget	£5.99		Quick Meals in Minutes	£5.99	
Dinner Beef	£5.99		Quick-mix Biscuits & Slices	£5.99	
Dinner Lamb (Sep 05)	£5.99		Quick-mix Cakes	£5.99	
Dinner Seafood	£5.99		Salads: Simple, Fast & Fresh	£5.99	
Easy Australian Style	£5.99		Saucery	£5.99	
Easy Curry	£5.99		Sensational Stir-Fries	£5.99	
Easy Spanish-Style	£5.99		Short-order Cook	£5.99	
Easy Vietnamese-Style	£5.99		Sweet Old Fashioned Favourites	£5.99	
Essential Barbecue	£5.99		Thai Cooking Class	£5.99	
Essential Microwave	£5.99		Vegetarian Meals in Minutes	£5.99	
Essential Soup	£5.99		Weekend Cook	£5.99	
Freezer, Meals from the	£5.99		Wicked Sweet Indulgences	£5.99	
French Cooking Class	£5.99		Wok, Meals in Minutes	£5.99	
			Total Cost:	**£**	

Mr/Mrs/Ms _____

Address _____

_____

Postcode _____ Country _____

Daytime phone (   ) _____

I enclose my cheque/money order

for £ _____

OR: please charge my

☐ Access   ☐ Visa   ☐ Mastercard

Cardholder's name _____

Card number

Expiry date ____ /____

Cardholder's signature _____

To order: Mail or fax – photocopy or complete the order form above, and send your credit card details or cheque payable to: Australian Consolidated Press (UK), Moulton Park Business Centre, Red House Road, Moulton Park, Northampton NN3 6AQ, phone (+44) (0) 1604 497531, fax (+44) (0) 1604 497533, e-mail books@acpuk.com

Non-UK residents: We accept the credit cards listed on the coupon, or cheques, drafts or International Money Orders payable in sterling and drawn on a UK bank. Credit card charges are at the exchange rate current at the time of payment.

Postage and packing: Within the UK, add £1.50 for one book or £3.00 for two books. There is no postal charge for orders of three or more books for delivery within the UK. For delivery outside the UK, please phone, fax or e-mail for a quote.

Offer ends 31.12.2005

Test Kitchen
Food director *Pamela Clark*
Associate food editors *Karen Hammial, Sue Wagner*
Home economists *Julie Ballard, Emma Braz, Christine Chandler, Kimberley Coverdale, Nadia French, Sarah Hobbs, Margaret Ientile, Amanda Kelly, Michelle Lawton, Kerrie Worner*
Editorial coordinator *Rebecca Steyns*
Stylists *Kay Francis, Sarah O'Brien*
Photographers *Alan Benson, Gerry Colley*

ACP Books
Editorial director *Susan Tomnay*
Creative director *Hieu Chi Nguyen*
Senior editor *Wendy Bryant*
Designer *Mary Keep*
Studio manager *Caryl Wiggins*
Editorial/sales coordinator *Caroline Lowry*
Editorial assistant *Karen Lai*
Publishing manager (sales) *Brian Cearnes*
Publishing manager (rights & new projects) *Jane Hazell*
Marketing manager *Sarah Cave*
Pre-press *Harry Palmer*
Production manager *Carol Currie*
Business manager *Seymour Cohen*
Assistant business analyst *Martin Howes*
Chief executive officer *John Alexander*
Group publisher *Pat Ingram*
Publisher *Sue Wannan*
Editor-in-chief *Deborah Thomas*

Produced by ACP Books, Sydney.
Printed by Dai Nippon Printing in Korea.
Published by ACP Publishing Pty Limited, 54 Park St, Sydney; GPO Box 4088, Sydney, NSW 2001.
Ph: (02) 9282 8618 Fax: (02) 9267 9438.
www.acpbooks.com.au
To order books, phone 136 116.
Send recipe enquiries to:
recipeenquiries@acp.com.au
AUSTRALIA: Distributed by Network Services GPO Box 4088, Sydney, NSW 2001.
Ph: (02) 9282 8777 Fax: (02) 9264 3278.
UNITED KINGDOM: Distributed by Australian Consolidated Press (UK), Moulton Park Business Centre, Red House Rd, Moulton Park, Northampton, NN3 6AQ.
Ph: (01604) 497 531 Fax: (01604) 497 533
acpukltd@aol.com
CANADA: Distributed by Whitecap Books Ltd 351 Lynn Ave, North Vancouver, BC, V7J 2C4
Ph: (604) 980 9852 Fax: (604) 980 8197
customerservice@whitecap.ca
www.whitecap.ca
NEW ZEALAND: Distributed by Netlink Distribution Company, ACP Media Centre, Cnr Fanshawe and Beaumont Streets, Westhaven, Auckland.
PO Box 47906, Ponsonby, Auckland, NZ.
Ph: (09) 366 9966 ask@ndcnz.co.nz

Clark, Pamela.
The Australian Women's Weekly Cooking Cl Chinese.

Includes index.
ISBN 1 86396434 7

© ACP Publishing Pty Limited 1978
ABN 18 053 273 546